Czechoslovak Armoured Fighting Vehicles

1918-1945

Czechoslovak Armoured Fighting Vehicles

1918-1945

Development for Czechoslovakia
Exploitation by Germany

Charles K. Kliment and Hilary Louis Doyle

BELLONA PUBLICATIONS
ARGUS BOOKS LTD,
ARGUS HOUSE,
14 ST JAMES RD.,
WATFORD,
HERTS.

*FRONT COVER: LT vz 35 tanks of the Czech Army. The three-man crew wore
one-pice overalls over regular uniforms. The licence number plates on front of
the vehicles are clearly visible. BACK COVER: The first of the Pz Kpfw 35(t)
impressed into German service (Bundesarchiv).*

Typeset by Inforum Ltd., Portsmouth
Printed in Great Britain by A. Wheaton & Co., Ltd., Exeter

Introduction

THIS work presents the history, development and war-time use of armoured fighting vehicles of Czechoslovak construction and manufacture both as broadly and with as much detail as possible. Czech armoured vehicles were of progressive construction. They were exported to many countries and played an important role in World War 2, expecially in the first two years.

Two of the Czech tanks were actually manufactured throughout the war years. ČKD's TNH P-S tank first as PzKpfw 38 (t), later, when no longer sufficient as a gun tank, became the basis for many self-propelled guns and soldiered on long after the war as a tank hunter and armoured personnel carrier. The Škoda T-22 tank was manufactured under licence in Hungary until 1944. Use was not limited to the Wehrmacht, besides Germany, Czech tanks were used by the armies of Bulgaria, Ethiopia, Hungary, Iran, Peru, Romania, Slovakia, Sweden, Switzerland and Yugoslavia.

Though the units of the Czechoslovak Army in exile were fighting with the Allies in the Middle East and Russia, Czech tanks and armoured fighting vehicles were fighting for the Germans and their Axis partners. Only late in 1944, after the volte-face of the Romanian army and the Slovak uprising, were they used on the Allied side.

Acknowledgements

The authors and publishers wish to thank the following for assistance in the production of this book: Mr Tom Jentz for his invaluable help in research; the Bundesarchiv, Koblenz; the Swedish Armour Association and ECPA.

ABOVE: PzKpfw 35(t) of the 6th Panzer Division in France, 1940. This Division and its forerunner, the 6th Panzer Brigade in Poland 1939, was the sole user of the PzKpfw 35(t). Note the detachable call sign plate on the rear of the vehicle. (Bundesarchiv).

Contents

1. Political Background

THE Czech countries, Bohemia and Moravia, obtained their independence from the Austro-Hungarian Empire in October 1918. They joined with Slovakia to form the Republic of Czechoslovakia.

The industrialization of the Czech countries had already got under way in the second half of the nineteenth century. During World War 1 they served as armament centers for the whole empire. After the liberation, most of this heavy industry remained in a comparatively small Czechoslovakia, which could not consume all the industry's output. It was vital to find new markets. Domestic designs for armoured fighting vehicles were developed and there was a strong impetus for their export.

During the twenties and continuing through the depression years the Czechoslovak Army was working on the proverbial shoestring. Exports were necessary to keep the armament factories going during these years. On the other hand, when the Army had sufficient funds and was placing large orders in the late thirties, because the danger of a new war was becoming real, it had to fight for allocation of production capacity in the factories.

This situation had its advantages and disadvantages. On one hand, the Army was able to exchange an old weapon for a new one by 'lending' the factories arms from its depots for an immediate export delivery, with the stipulation that the factories would replace the older weapon with a better or an improved model. This situation was fairly common in the small arms field, and as will be shown later, was practised even in tank exports.

On the other hand, even in the criticial days before the Munich agreement in 1938, some armament factories were giving to the export orders the same priority as Army orders, and tanks and arms were exported even though the army did not have enough of them.

Though the Czechoslovak Army was modernizing its thinking and equipment, it remained heavily dependent on the horse up to 1939. This was for two reasons: the limited capacity of the car and truck manufacturers and political reasons. In pre-war Czechoslovakia the political party representing the farmers was always one of the most influential, and it was felt that the Army should use as many horses as possible.

Czechoslovakia ceased to exist as a free state on 15 March, 1939 when the Germans occupied Bohemia and Moravia and incorporated them as a Protectorate into the Third Reich. Slovakia was allowed to form a Slovak State which retained certain independence, though it was closely allied with Germany.

ABOVE: A company of Swedish Strv m/37 on exercise. Built by Oskarsham they were the Swedish version of ČKD's AH-IV Sv. These machines served during World War 2, although delegated to reconnaissance only.

All the arms and equipment of the Czechoslovak Army were confiscated by the Germans excepting the units stationed on the soil of Slovakia. These units, including their equipment, were retained by the Slovak Free State.

The industry in the Protectorate was either put under German control or made a part of German industrial concerns. During the entire war it continued turning out arms and equipment for the German forces, including tanks.

BELOW: After being pulled off the front line duty, the PzKpfw 38(t) soldiered up to the end of the war in anti-partisan duties and as parts of armoured trains. Riding on special flat-bed cars, they could quickly disembark on special ramps and lead counter-attacks away from the tracks.

2. The Manufacturers

THE famous Škoda works in Pilsen in the Western part of Bohemia opened their modern steel works in 1886 and in 1890 founded their armament department. They quickly became the sole supplier of heavy naval and fortress guns for the Austro-Hungarian navy and army. At the beginning of this century, they started manufacturing field guns as well. After World War 1, Škoda was exporting their guns all over the world and therefore were in an excellent position when dealing with the representatives of the military.

Though Škoda owned the largest car manufacturing facilities in Czecho-slovakia, having bought the famous Laurin & Klement factory, they were not interested in the tank manufacture from the start, supplying the Army as they were with armoured cars. But when the Army accepted and ordered the development of the Tančik vz 33 tankette and the LT vz 34 tank from their competitors, the ČKD (Praga), Škoda was quick to realize how lucrative a business tanks represented. From 1930 to 1932 Škoda began sending proposals for tanks to the Army to show their capability of designing and manufacturing tanks. In February 1933 they submitted to an Army commision their two tankettes, the S-I (MUV-4; Malý Útočný Vuz; small attack vehicle) and S-I-P. As the Army at this time already had the ČKD tankette ordered, it only promised to test the Škoda vehicles.

BELOW: The Tančik vz 33 of 1933, not a particularly good design as on some tests its armour was penetrated by rifle bullets!

A very interesting development of the Škoda tankettes appeared in 1934. Škoda at this time had finished the development of their Z 1 gun, suitable both as an anti-aircraft and anti-tank gun. The 4 cm gun (L/71) had a muzzle velocity of 950 m/sec and with an anti-tank shell was efficient against a 30 mm armour up to 2,500 m. Škoda developed armour-piercing and HE shells for this gun, which was effective against aircraft up to 4,000 m.

The gun was placed in an open-top superstructure of 12 mm armour on the improved MUV-4 tankette, which was now designated MU-6. The combination tipped the scale at 4.2 t and with a 6 cylinder 'Boxer' engine was capable of speeds up to 40 km/hour. The main advantage of the combination was the ease with which the very efficient gun could have been brought to the ready position and against both tanks and aircraft. This construction was way ahead of its time, the only comparable vehicle being the Hungarian Nimrod self-propelled gun, which appeared several years later.

Unfortunately the Czechoslovak Army was not interested, and this development remained a prototype, and the army continued to be desperately short of both anti-tank and anti-aircraft weapons up to 1939.

In February 1934 Škoda, realizing that tankettes were neither successful nor popular, and that the next step would inevitably be a real tank, called the

Škoda self-propelled gun of 1934. At this time, the 4 cm Z1 gun was deadly against any contemporary tank. This is the anti-tank configuration.

ABOVE: Superstructure of the MU 6 carrier in the open position for anti-aircraft fire. This was a fast mobile platform with an excellent gun and was a very advanced combination for its day.

Army commision again. Škoda presented to the commision their medium tank SU in three mock-ups. One of them was actually manufactured as a prototype and bought by the Army, but was not adopted for production.

Nevertheless, Škoda proceeded full speed with a better, improved construction, the S-II-a tank. The Škoda representatives exerted pressure in the proper army circles to get the orders for this model. A mock-up was presented to an Army commision in October 1934 and the test of two prototypes was performed in June 1935. Though the results of these tests were not very favourable and showed that the design was not yet perfected, the influence and prestige of Škoda finally prevailed and an order for 160 tanks of the S-II-a type was placed on 30 October, 1935, and this was followed with an additional 138 tanks in 1937. Another batch of 126 tanks were ordered for export to Romania in 1936.

The Army got sufficient funds to order more tanks in 1937. But this time, however, even the influence of Škoda was not sufficient to offset all the troubles the Armoured Corps were experiencing with their tanks. The Army decided to run a proper comparative test of all the new constructions. Škoda

ABOVE: Crews manning the vz 33 tankettes and the OA vz 30 armoured cars. These tankette were badly protected, riding in them was very tiring and the incidence of defects was high. The crews disliked them and the armoured corps gladly transferred them to the infantry divisions to be used as recce vehicles.

entries were proven inferior to ČKD's and thus their position as a tank supplier to the Army was ended.

Undaunted, Škoda turned their interest to exports. In 1938 the S-II-a tanks were demonstrated to a commision of the Red Army, but the Russians were not interested. (The Red Army had been buying Škoda guns for some time, and therefore Škoda had good contacts with them). Another order for Afghanistan did not materialize either. But in October 1938 Škoda officially asked the Ministry of Defense for a clearance to sell quite a significant number of weapons to Britain. A part of the list were S-II-a tanks, and Škoda asked the Army to lend them tanks for this order (up to 100 tanks were called for) with a provision that Škoda would replace them with either an improved model of the S-II-a tank or with the new ČKD TNH tanks. The Ministry of Defense originally accepted this proposal, but in December 1938 permission was withdrawn. Škoda persisted up to February 1939, when during the final meeting with the Army representatives, the proposal was definitively turned down.

When their S-III medium tank was scrapped in early 1937, Škoda designers began working on another project. Started as another light tank, it gradually grew into a medium. This explains its untypical designation S-II-c. Not ready for the 1938 trials, it was further developed into the T-21, followed by improved an uparmoured models T-22 and T-23.

Českomoravska-Kolben-Daněk (ČKD), as the name implies, was formed by a merger of old established engineering firms. Gradually, as the concern

ABOVE: Škoda adapted, in 1919, twelve Fiat Torino truck chassis to armoured cars. High and heavy, they were confined to roads only. Two Schwarzlose heavy machine-guns in two separate turrets had a 360° field of fire.

grew in size and power, it acquired other companies. One of these was the Praga works, makers of trucks, tractors and passenger cars. Most of the ČKD factories were situated in Prague.

ČKD was not an armaments manufacturer, but was supplying the Army with trucks and artillery tractors. They were ideally suited for tank production and were quick to seize the opportunity when the Army was looking for a manufacturer for tankettes. Their tankette design, designated P-I, which was a modification of the Carden-Lloyd tankette, was not very successful, though the Army finally ordered 70 in 1933 as the Tančik vz 33.

Even during its development ČKD was not very happy with the tankette and immediately on their own initiative started the development of a light tank, the P-II. It had a Škoda 37 mm anti-tank gun in a fully revolving turret and two machine guns. Though it had some shortcomings, it was a dependable, simple and rugged vehicle. The Army bought 50 of them in 1934.

As was already recounted, Škoda broke through the ČKD hegemony in 1935 with their S-II-a tank and deprived ČKD of any further Army contracts. ČKD at this time were already perfecting their two new models, the AH-IV and TNH light tanks. As the domestic market was now closed to them, they started an export drive to sell these tanks to many countries. At the same time, since Škoda did not have the capacity to fulfill both the domestic and export orders, Škoda and ČKD entered into a production agreement with ČKD manufacturing the S-II-a tanks was well. Continual changes on these tanks, made by both Škoda and ČKD engineering teams,

11

ABOVE: The Kolohousenka (wheel-cum-track) KH 50 was an unwieldy design which was never really successful, though Škoda spent several years with Tatra on the project. The vehicle carried its own ramps for the track-to-wheel change, which took about ten minutes of strenuous labour for the crew. BELOW, LEFT AND RIGHT: The change from wheels to track.

were not always coordinated or even passed on to the other company. This made both the manufacturers unhappy and the Army was especially displeased with the state of affairs. ČKD finally, in 1937, refused to participate in future manufacturing of the Škoda tanks, as they were tooling up for their new designs.

ČKD won the 1938 Army trials with their two entries. The TNH P-S tank which was fully developed after three years of manufacture for export proved to be an excellent and dependable vehicle. The new medium tank V-8-H while not proven was chosen as a standard medium tank for the Army.

Shortly after the TNH P-S tank was accepted as the LT vz 38, the Army ordered, in 1938, 150 tanks to be made as soon as possible. The first 20 vehicles were supposed to be delivered before the end of 1938 and the remaining 130 before the end of May, 1939. The production of the V-8-H mediums as the ST vz 39 was planned at 20 vehicles a month for a total cf 300 to be completed by March 1940. After the Munich Agreement all the special emergency appropriations were revoked and the production was slowed down considerably.

ČKD offered the TNH P-S tank to Britain practically at the same time as Škoda did their S-II-a. In February, 1939, ČKD asked the Ministry of Defense for approval to send one TNH P-S tank for trials to Britain and to sell the license for manufacturing this model. In the same month, they got the approval to show not only the TNH P-S tank, but the V-8-H as well. Both tanks were presented to British experts in Prague and the Ministry of Defense approved the lending of the 37 mm gun and the two machine-guns for the TNH P-S tank. This tank was shipped for testing in the U.K. in March 1939, but the final agreement was never reached because the German occupation of Czechoslovakia took place the same month.

The first nine TNH P-S tanks were delivered on 22 May, 1939, after the German occupation and no production V-8-H tanks were manufactured at all. Not only was the production of the 150 TNH P-S tanks retained by Germany but they subsequently continued production of this tank and its derivations up to 1945.

In the years preceeding 1939 ČKD also developed some interesting prototypes, but none of them was ever manufactured.

The armour plates for all AFV's were manufactured by the Poldi steel works in Kladno, both in homogenous plate and in face-hardened armour plate. All the guns were manufactured by Škoda, while the machine-guns were the product of Zbrojovka Brno.

Tatra, the third manufacturer, is of far less significance than Škoda or ČKD. Tatra works in Kopřivnice in Moravia were the manufacturers of railway rolling stock, trucks, buses, tractors and cars. They originally cooperated with Škoda on the wheel-cum-track designs and produced some artillery tractors of this type. Their only construction accepted by the Czech

ABOVE: The Tatra OA vz 30 were fast and manoeuvrable, but very lightly armoured and armed with only light machine-guns vz 26. Moreover, they carried no radio.

army was the 1930 Tatra 72 armoured car, OA vz 30. Though they had an interesting prototype of a 260 HP tank engine of radial design, they did not play any role in tank design or manufacture although during the German occupation Tatra were responsible for several engines used in fighting vehicles.

Designation of Armoured Fighting Vehicles

All the Czech armoured fighting vehicles were officially to have two designations, a factory designation and, after acceptance, the Army designation.

The factory designations were to be as follows:

S = Škoda   P = (Praga) ČKD (Českomoravska Kolben Danek)
I = tankette   II = light tank   III = medium tank

Suffix -a- designated a cavalry tank, while suffix -b- designated an uparmoured and upgunned infantry version. So for example S-II-a was Škoda light tank, cavalry version.

There were some exceptions to this rule as the need arose to identify numerous versions. For example the S-II-c tank, which as a medium tank should also have been designated S-III, or the S-I-d tankette, where the -d-meant *Delovy* (gun).

Praga abandoned these designations after their P-II tank. As their subsequent constructions were made for export only, they used untypical designations like AH-IV or TNH. The succeeding export versions had different designations again, like LTP, LTH etc, where LT meant Light Tank (*Lehky Tank* in Czech) and the last letter designated the country of destination.

Škoda changed their designations in 1940 for a T-number series, starting with T-1 and ending with T-25. A cross-reference to all these designations is in Table 1.

Armoured cars were designated by Škoda as PA (*Pancerove Auto*: armoured car) and a Roman numeral, like PA-I, PA-II etc, whilst Tatra used their normal factory model number designation, like Tatra 34, Tatra 72, etc.

If an armoured fighting vehicle was accepted by the Army, it got the official Army designation. Its first two letters designated the category, for example OA (*Obrneny Automobil*: armoured car), LT (*Lehky Tank*: Light

Table 1: AFV Designations

Manu-facturer	Type of Vehicle	Manufacturer's Designation	Czech Army Designation	Export
Škoda	armoured car	PA-I	–	
	armoured car	PA-II	OA vz 25	M-25 (Austria)
	armoured car	PA-III	OA vz 27	
	armoured car	PA-II·75	OA vz 29	
	tankette	MUV-4 S-I/T-1	–	
	tankette	S-I-P/T-2	–	
	tankette	S-I-D/T-2D	–	
	tankette	T-3D	–	T-32 (Yugoslavia)
	light tank	S-II-a/T-11	LT vz 35	R-2 (Romania) LT vz 35 (Slovakia) PzKpfw 35(t) (Germany) (Bulgaria)
	light tank (47 mm gun)	S-II-a/T-12	–	
	light tank (37 mm gun)	S-II-b/T-13	–	
	light tank (47 mm gun)	S-II-b/T-14	–	
	light tank (recce)	T-15	–	Pz Spah wg II Ausf Škoda
	medium tank	SU	–	
	medium tank	S-III	–	
	medium tank	S-II-c/T-21	–	
	medium tank	T-22	–	40 M Turán közhk (Hungary)
	medium tank	T-23	–	

Manu-facturer	Type of Vehicle	Manufacturer's Designation	Czech Army Designation	Export
Tatra	armoured car	Type 72	OA vz 30	OA vz 30 (Slovakia)
ČKD (Praga)	tankette	P-I	Tancik vz 33	Tancik vz 33 (Slovakia)
	light tank	P-II	LT vz 34	
	light tank	AH-IV	–	R-1 (Romania)
	light tank	AH-IV	–	RH (Iran)
	light tank	AH-IV Sv	–	Strv m/37 (Sweden)
	light tank	AH-IV	–	(Ethiopia)
	light tank	F-IV-H	–	
	light tank	LTP	–	(Peru)
	light tank	LTH	–	Pz 39 (Switzerland)
	light tank	LTL	–	(Latvia)
	light tank		–	LT vz 40 (Slovakia)
	light tank	TNH	–	TNH (Iran)
	light tank	TNHP-S	LT vz 38	PzKpfw 38(t) (Germany) LT vz 38 (Slovakia) 38M(t) k hk (Hungary) (Romania) (Bulgaria)
	light tank	TNH Sv	–	Strv m/41 (Sweden)
	light tank (recce)	TNHnA	–	PzSpah wg II Ausf BMM (Germany)
	medium tank	V-8-H	ST vz 39	–

tank) or ST (*Středni Tank*: medium tank). The letters were followed by 'vz' (*Vzor*; Mark) and the last two numerals of the year of introduction into service. So for example we have LT vz 35 which was the S-II-a, LT vz 38 which was the TNH P-S, ST vz 39 was the V-8-H, OA vz 27 was the PA-III and OA vz 30 was the Tatra 72, and so on.

3. Doctrine of the Czechoslovak Army

AFTER World War 1 the Army's officers were recruited from the cadres of the old Austro-Hungarian army and from officers who fought in the Legions. These were men who saw their real duty as fighting against the Austro-Hungarian forces with the Allies for the liberation of Czechoslovakia. There were three such legions: French, Italian and Russian. These people brought different views, depending on the army they fought in. In the end, however, the French military doctrine prevailed. For many years the French Army maintained a military mission with the general staff of the Czechoslovak Army.

The Army soon learned the importance of armoured fighting vehicles when it used the armoured trains inherited from the Austro-Hungarians and two Lancia armoured cars of the Italian Legion in the fighting against communist Hungary in 1919. Recognizing the need for a specialized force,

BELOW: The Ansaldo-Lancia armoured car, one of two the Italian Legion brought home with them after 1918. It weighed 3.8 tons, armour was 6 mm and it carried 2 machine-guns in a fully rotating turret. Maximum speed was 70 km/hour, crew 6 men. These cars were used in the fighting against communist Hungary in 1919.

ABOVE: The LT vz 34 was the last ČKD light tank using multiple small wheel suspension. With an only 62 hp engine, it was slightly underpowered.

the 'Special Fighting Forces' were initiated in 1920 and these were converted to Armoured Corps in 1922.

General Pellé, the head of the French military mission, proposed that the armoured corps should be equipped with light French Renault tanks. Because the neighbouring Poles bought 150 of these machines, there was some concern that the Army should be equipped with tanks as soon as possible. But due to the limited financial means of the Army and plans for domestic production of armoured fighting vehicles only seven of the Renaults were bought and used for training.

In 1926 finance was forthcoming and the first specification for a tank prototype was drawn up. The tank was to have a maximum weight of 10 metric tons, speed between 15 and 25 km per hour, armour sufficient to stop rifle and machine-gun bullets and shell fragments, 3 man crew, endurance 6—8 hours and armament of one 75 mm gun and two machine-guns in a fully rotating turret. It was to be capable of fording up to 0.8 m, crossing trenches two meters wide and climbing up to 45 degrees. It took seven years before a tank with corresponding parameters could be developed and then only with a smaller 37 mm gun.

The Army's thinking was instead diverted to two armoured vehicle concepts which influenced the thinking of nearly all the general staffs of that period. One was the wheel-cum-track vehicle, the other the tankette.

Wheel-cum-track vehicles were favoured over tanks because of the inferior construction of the running gear and especially the track of contemporary fully tracked tanks, whose radius of action was therefore very limited. If the tanks could use wheels on good roads to get to the fighting zone and there change to tracks, they would arrive much more quickly and in a fresh condition. Several prototypes of these vehicles were being developed by various companies for over six years, but none of them was successful enough to warrant production.

The tankette concept, based on Fuller's theories, was followed with great interest. The main advantage was the ease of manufacture and the low price of these vehicles. Their operational and tactical deficiencies were mainly overlooked. The Army was actually equipped with tankettes of Czech manufacture in 1933, Tančik vz 33, but these only showed that the tankette, as a fighting vehicle, had a very limited value.

In 1934 the tank won its place with the introduction of the light tank LT vz 34, followed a year later with the LT vz 35. Both were light, fast and maneuvrable, armed with a 37 mm tank gun and two machine-guns. Far better constructions of both light and medium tanks were available in 1938, but none of them was brought to production before the German occupation.

In the thirties, the doctrine of the Army crystallized. The French influence was probably paramount in the decision to build a ring of fortifications on the borders with Germany. These were formidable underground forts, connected with several lines of pill-boxes. Like the Maginot Line, they were supposed to break the first impetus of the attack and allow for the reserves to be brought forward. The armoured fighting vehicles, however, contrary to the French doctrine, were not tied to the infantry and subjugated piecemeal into infantry divisions. Instead, the highly mobile gun tanks were concentrated into 'Fast Divisions'.

These Divisions were a combination of tanks, cavalry and motorized infantry units. Each had two brigades of cavalry, two battalions of tanks (114 tanks total), two regiments of motorized infantry on trucks, one regiment of cyclists, two artillery batallions (one motorized, one horse-drawn), one anti-aircraft and one anti-tank company and supporting units. Total strength of the Division was 10,500 men and 460 officers. There were four such Divisions in the 1938 mobilization.

It should be emphasized that the cavalry units of these 'Fast Divisions' were not the cavalry in the old sense, as for example in the Polish Army. These units were trained to fight as dragoons: dismounted, and were equipped like infantry with machine-guns, mortars and anti-tank guns carried dismantled on the horses. Thus, the horse was envisaged only as a means of transport with unlimited cross-country capability.

The 'Fast Divisions' were in the Army reserve to be used as a strong supporting force in a case of an enemy's breakthrough, or as a spearhead for

ABOVE: Small detached tank units were used during 1938 to help quench the German Freikorps activities in the Sudetenland. These LT vz 35 tanks were supplied by the 'Fast Divisions'.

offensive action. The rest of the available armoured fighting vehicles, like the armoured cars and the tankettes, were used by the infantry divisions as reconnaissance and supporting units. Each Infantry Division had a platoon of tanks (three vehicles, either Tančik vz 33 or LT vz 34) in a 'Mixed Reconnaissance Unit'.

Organization of Armoured Units of the Czechoslovak Army

Infantry Divisions:
Each Infantry Division had a 'Mixed Reconnaissance Unit', which had a platoon of light tanks (3 Tančik vz 33). During the 1938 mobilization there were 22 Infantry Divisions, with 66 Tancik vz 33.

Border Areas:
There were twelve Border Areas (on Corps level). Each area had one platoon of light tanks (3 LT vz 34 or Tančik vz 33). There were six platoons of armoured cars, which were used according to the needs of each area, in all 24 armoured cars.

Armoured Corps Regiments:
In peace-time the tanks were concentrated in Armoured Corps Regiments. There were four such regiments, 1st based at Milovice, 2nd based at Vyškov, 3rd based at Martin and the 4th based at Pardubice. The 4th Armoured Corps Regiment was forming in 1938 and was slated to get the new LT vz 38. 1st Armoured Corps Regiment was the main one (Milovice being the tank training ground serving as the equivalent of Bovington in Britain, Aberdeen in the USA or Sennelager in Germany). In 1937 the 1st Armoured Corps Regiment had one batallion of light tanks and one batallion of armoured cars, in winter 1937/8 two more tank batallions and one armoured car batallion were added. During the 1938 mobilization it supplied four tank batallions to the 'Fast Divisions'.

The Armoured Corps Regiments were planned to supply two light tank batallions, one company of armoured cars and one additional company of light tanks to the corresponding 'Fast Division' (ie 1st Armoured Corps Regiment was to equip the 1st Fast Division, etc).

'Fast Divisions'
The four 'Fast Divisions' were located as follows:

Unit	Formed in	Headquarters
1st	Praha	Pacov
2nd	Brno	Jaroměřice
3rd	Nové Zámky	Levice
4th	Pardubice	Soběslav

During the 1938 mobilization, the 'Fast Divisions' had only one tank batallion each, as the tanks which were loaned to the Border Areas did not come back in time. In any case, the Army did not have enough tanks to equip all the 'Fast Divisions'. The tank batallion had 49 tanks, made up of three tank companies, each with 16 tanks, and one command tank. However, it was planned that each 'Fast Division' theoretically would have had 114 tanks of the LT vz 35 or LT vz 38 type, two tank batallions and one tank

21

ABOVE: Two LT vz 35 during the Summer 1938 field manoeuvres. Standard three-tone camouflage pattern was ochre, brown and grass green applied over the original khaki base paint. Czechoslovak army tanks did not carry any unit or code signs but used pennant and hand signals for control.

company. Of the planned number (total for four 'Fast Divisions' 456 tanks) only 298 LT vz 35 were available by 1939.

Total planned armoured vehicles	Tanks	Armoured Cars
Infantry Divisions	66 Tančik vz 33	–
Border Areas	36 LT vz 34	24 OA vz 27
'Fast Divisions'	456 LT vz 38, 35, 34	48 OA vz 30
Total required	558 LT	72 OA
Available	428 LT	75 OA

Camouflage and Markings of Czechoslovak Armoured Fighting Vehicles

All the armoured fighting vehicles delivered to the Army were painted olive drab by the manufacturer. The French-type three-tone camouflage of

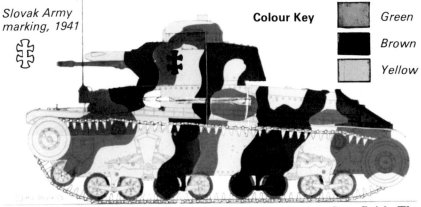

Slovak Army marking, 1941

Colour Key

Green

Brown

Yellow

LT vz 35 of the Czechoslovak Army, 1938 in standard camouflage finish. The Slovaks simply added their marking.

irregular patches of ochre, green and brown was applied by the units for special occasions like field exercises etc.

Whilst in pre-war Czechoslovak service the only markings carried on front and back plates was a licence number, white on black plate with white border. It consisted of five digits. For special and armoured vehicles the first two digits were always 13 followed by a three digit vehicle number.

Czechoslovak Army Licence Number System – AFVs and Special Vehicles

Vehicle	Designation	Number Built	Identified Numbers
Škoda Z Artillery tractor	vz 20	106	13.245, 247
Breitfeld-Daněk 25PS Artillery tractor			13.313, 314
Škoda PA-III Armoured car	OA vz 27	27	13.342, 343, 347
Tatra 72 Armoured car	OA vz 30	51	13.376, 377, 380, 384, 386, 389, 390
ČKD P-I Tankette	Tančik vz 33	70	13.420, 421, 430
ČKD P-II light tank	LT vz 34	50	13.533

BELOW: LT vz 35 tanks during exercise in the standard pre-war three-tone camouflage and with the AFV special licence plate well shown. Though of advanced design the tanks were plagued by continuous malfunctions of the pneumatic gear-changing system. Note rubber mud-flaps on the front of fenders.

ABOVE AND BELOW: LT vz 35 tanks of the 'Slovak Fast Division' before Barbarossa. Inherited from the Czechoslovak Army, they retained the camouflage scheme and the licence number plates. German style white call sign numbers and the Slovak cross were added on the turret.

Škoda MTH Artillery tractor		54	13.599, 602
Škoda S-II-a	LT vz 35	298	13.666, 676, 678, 685, 689, 13.719, 722, 13.846, 847, 870, 894, 898, 899, 13.900, 909, 939

ABOVE: An LT vz 40 command tank. The LT vz 40 turret had a different shape as compared with the 38(t) series. Commander's cupola was cast with no periscopes and was part of the left half of the hatch. Carrying the original National insignia, the white double cross of Slovakia.

BELOW: LT vz 38 PzKpfw 38(t) Ausf S of the Slovak Army. Following the German example, four-man crews were carried. The soldiers are wearing the pre-war Czechoslovak Army uniforms and overalls. National Insignia on the turret is the blue-white-red shield which was used from 1942.

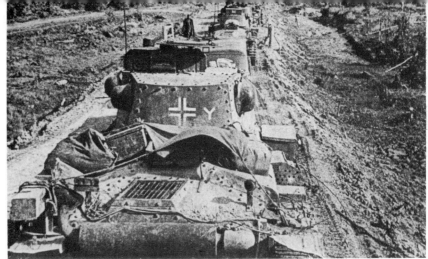

ABOVE: PzKpfw 38(t) carrying the Divisional sign of 7th Panzer Division in Russia, 1941. Panzer Regiment 25 of this Division had the single greatest concentration of PzKpfw 38(t) — 174 tanks including 7 Command.

Sometime after the formation of the Slovak Free State Czech AFVs still serving with the Slovak 'Fast Division' had either German style turret call sign numbers added with the white 'double cross' of Slovakia or the cross alone was carried.

At a slightly later date the National insignia of a blue-white-red shield was carried, normally without a call sign number.

All Czech vehicles in Germany Army service were given a base coating of

RIGHT: Pz BefWg 38(t), or Befehlspanzer (Command tank), in France 1940 with the 7th Panzer Division. Each division had between 7 and 10 command tanks, which were very conspicuous with their long range frame antenna. Note the outline style cross and, unusually, the Signals tac mark.

*Overall grey
with white
solid cross*

Pz Kpfw 38(t) Ausf A Panzer Abteilung 67, 3rd Leichte Division, Poland, September, 1939.

*Overall grey with white
call sign numbers and
outline style cross. (Yellow
Divisional sign of IV Pz
Div. shown).*

Pz Kpfw 38(t) Ausf C standard markings, 1940–1941.

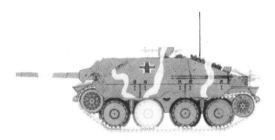

Jagdpanzer 38(t) Hetzer.Typical camouflage scheme, 1945.

*Overall yellow with
black, outlined white cross*

7.5 cm PaK 40/3 auf Pz Kpfw 38(t) Ausf H standard camouflage scheme, 1943.

red oxide primer, which was rust coloured, during manufacture. Factory finished vehicles were normally sprayed in a single colour. Any additional colours for camouflage purposes were applied by the units. The following colours were standardised:

Earth Brown RAL 8020; Field Gray RAL 7008; Dark Grey RAL 7027. From 1935 – 40 vehicles could be seen either in one of these single colours, or RAL 8020 combined with one of the other two in a disruptive pattern. In 1941 application of a fourth basic colour started for vehicles sent to North Africa; this was Sand Brown RAL 8000. This was used either on its own or with a mottle application applied from one of the other colours.

From February 18, 1943, a new system came into effect whereby the previous colours were replaced by a single overall colour of Middle Sand (Mittelsand) applied at the factory. A kit of water based soluble paints in paste form was issued with each tank consisting of the following colours: Olive Green, Red Brown, Dark Yellow and White, 2 kg of each. This was mixed with water or petrol and applied by spray gun or brush to suit operational conditions. White water based paint had been issued from 1941 as a camouflage for cold weather theatres, such as the Russian front. It was possible to vary the colour scheme from day to day if required. Use was also made of captured Allied paint stocks in theatres where these were available.

National insignia was a plain white cross applied for the Polish campaign of 1939. This showed to the rear, front, sides, and top. Thereafter a black cross with white outline was used, similar to that used on aircraft. Sometimes, particularly later in the war, only a white outline type of cross was used. The cross normally showed to the rear and sides only and was painted on the hull or superstructure. For air recognition a German national flag was normally used on turret or superstructure top, but local use was also made of coloured cloth panels to suit operational requirements.

The first three panzer divisions adopted 'traditional' formation signs related to their origin; for example 3.Pz-Div. had the brown bear of Berlin.

BELOW: The R-2 at the Dnjestr in 1941. The white Romanian crosses were carried on front sides and on top of the engine cover. Large call signs on the turret followed German practice.

ABOVE: Marshall Model and General Lakatos inspect a Turan I company at Stanislawo, 1944. From 1942 the Hungarian Army used white crosses on a black square for recognition and white call signs.

From 1939 however, formalised runic formation signs were ordered for all panzer divisions and these were painted in white, yellow, or black (depending on background colour) on the front and rear of each vehicle (usually left front and right rear but much depended on the vehicle or unit). In 1941 there was a change of allocation of these formation signs. In some cases the senior divisions also displayed their pre-1939 formation signs or other non-runic signs. Some vehicles or units also carried individual markings, notably company markings, but the form of these greatly varied. Some tanks indicated 'kills' by white bands painted round the barrel.

The tactical sign of a tank was its turret number. Until 1940, the vehicles tactical number was painted on a detachable rhomboidshaped plate (itself the tactical symbol for a tank) and this was clipped to the vehicle to show to the sides and rear. Thereafter the number was more usually painted in large digits on the turret sides, either in 'solid' or white-outlined form. The large numbers were adopted as a result of war experience and enabled a unit commander to quickly call up one of his vehicles by radio and pick it out more easily across the battlefield. The number was painted to show to the sides and rear. The three digits signified the *Kompanie* (first digit), the *Zug* (platoon) (second digit), and individual vehicle in the platoon.

Command tanks (which included staff tanks, e.g. adjutant) were marked with R for the regimental command staff, R01 would be the regimental commander, followed by R02, R03, etc. allocated to other command staff officers. Battalion staff vehicles were indicated by the Roman numeral I for the first battalion, and II for the second battalion (abteilung) within a regiment.

Vehicles in Romanian service were olive drab with a white Romanian cross and German style call signs.

Hungarian Army units originally used a red cross outlined white on a diagonal green square. Later they followed the German Army practice with white crosses on a black square as their National marking.

4. History and Development of Operational AFVs

Armoured Cars

WHEN the Czechoslovak Army was organized in 1918, it had several armoured trains and two Lancia armoured cars. As there was a pressing needs for more armoured cars, Škoda built an armoured body on a commercial Fiat Torino truck chassis. Twelve of the high and unwieldy cars with two machine-gun turrets were on the inventory of the Army up to 1929.

In 1922 an Army order for a development of a specialized armoured car was placed with Škoda. The first two prototypes of the PA-I Škoda finished in 1923. The car had a turret with two machine-guns, four-wheel drive and could be driven in both directions. The Army did not accept it, because it was too high and had low stability. Škoda reworked the car in two weeks in a highly original manner. The turret was removed, all armour surfaces were slanted and rounded and the car was armed with four machine-guns in special ball mountings, which allowed a 360 degrees field of fire. The car retained the four wheel drive and again could be driven in both directions. This was the famous PA-II Turtle, considered by many to be the most modern armoured car of its time. The Army bought twelve of these cars and designated them OA vz 25. They were used up to 1934, when three were sold to the Vienna police. The Austrians later modified them by adding a small observation cupola for the commander. One such vehicle survived up to the end of World War 2.

Since the armoured cars were originally envisaged as support vehicles for infantry, a heavier armament than machine-guns was planned. Škoda modified one of the PA-II cars by installing the 75 mm field gun into the front plate. Only one machine-gun in the back was retained. Though the Army bought this prototype and even gave it the OA vz 29 designation, it was not accepted for production, as it was too heavy and slow, with practically no cross-country capability.

Škoda introduced their heavy armoured car, the PA-III, in July 1927. The car was accepted by the Army as OA vz 27 and was retained up to 1939. Originally it was armed with two machine-guns in a fully rotating turret while heavier armament was planned to enable it to act as a support vehicle.

ABOVE: The famous Škoda 'Turtle', designated OA vz 25 in Army service. The balistically very effective hull was expensive to manufacture. Four Schwarzlose heavy machine-guns provided 360° coverage, but their water cooling jackets were vulnerable to small arms fire. This vehicle sports the three-tone camouflage applied for manoeuvres, and an old licence number plate. The new licence numbering system was only adopted starting with the OA vz 27 armoured car.

Plans comprised of the installation of either a 14.5 mm heavy machine-gun or a 37 mm gun, but as the emphasis shifted to tanks, this was never realized.

Tatra was supplying the Army with armoured trucks as personnel carriers and so it was only natural that they should start developing armoured cars as well. Their armoured car Tatra 34 from 1929 was not accepted by the Army, but the Tatra 72 was accepted as OA vz 30 and ordered into production. It represented a departure from the four-wheel drive Škoda cars, driveable in both directions, as it had a conventional light truck chassis. But it was light,

RIGHT: In 1934, the Army retired the OA vz 25 armoured cars and sold several to the Vienna police, who used them on several occasions to quell riots. In Austrian service, a small oberservation cupola for the commander was added.

LEFT: Tatra OA vz 30, light recce armoured car. One example was sent to France to the Société Genérale Aeronautique for demonstration to the French General Staff in 1934. However, nothing further came of this.

BELOW: Zbrojovka Brno was the smallest car manufacturer in pre-war Czechoslovakia, its main production effort being in the small arms field. But it produced several good models. The Z-car was an adaptation of one of them to a lightly armoured scout car. Armament was one ZB vz 27 machine-gun.

ABOVE: ČKD did not join in the development of armoured cars, however, they did produce some armoured vehicles, based on their Praga truck chassis, for use by Police units.

with an air-cooled engine, and owing to the central tube chassis with swinging half-axles, had good cross-country capabilities. As it was meant for reconnaissance only, it was armed with two light machine-guns, one in front plate, one in the fully rotating turret.

As already mentioned, the wheel-cum-track concept was in great favour with the Army in the late twenties. Starting in 1924, Škoda cooperated with Tatra on the 'Kolohousenka' series. The first vehicle, KH 50, was produced in 1925, KH 60 in 1928 and KH 70 in 1930. All these models used the mechanical change from wheels to track and carried their own ramps to effect this change, which required about ten minutes. In all, they were not successful and were used for driver training only. The KH 70 armoured vehicle was sold to Turkey and can be found in the German Recognition Manuals from 1939.

Tanks

In 1930 the Army decided to buy three Carden Lloyd tankettes and asked ČKD to develop one of their own. It was envisaged that they would be tested side-by-side and the better vehicle ordered. In the same year ČKD built three P-I vehicles and tested them extensively. All the known shortcomings of the tankette P-I became apparent during these tests. Nevertheless, in 1933 70 vehicles of this type were ordered and delivered. They were designated Tančik vz 33 by the Army. Their users in the Army decried them most vehemently for the high incidence of break-downs, restricted vision and poor riding characteristics, which caused excessive fatigue of the crews.

Despite all this, the tankettes were still in use in 1939, though relegated to infantry divisions as reconnaissance vehicles.

ČKD, aware of the shortcomings of tankettes and their P-I, started a development of a light tank side-by-side with the manufacture of the P-I. This tank, the P-II, carried a 37 mm anti-tank gun in a fully rotating turret. The Army were impressed and ordered 50 tanks of this type and designated them LT vz 34. It was a good vehicle, with a low incidence of breakdowns and easy maintenance. During the tests it covered over four thousand kilometers without any major break-down. Though the tank had some shortcomings, like tiring steering and excessive noise level, and the gun was not fully suitable for turret use, being an adapted Škoda anti-tank gun, it was a sound vehicle and soldiered faithfully up to 1939. Most of its shortcomings were eliminated during the 1938 reconstruction programme. The ČKD team of designers, under the direction of Dipl.Ing. Alexander Surin, had been working on new tank designs. But the hegemony of ČKD as a sole tank supplier to the Army was shattered by Škoda in 1934.

Škoda was aware that owing to the changing international situation, especially in Germany, the Army would start a rearmament programme very soon. And they certainly did not want to let ČKD get the contracts. In 1933 the last wheel-cum-track project was stopped. Škoda immediately asked the Army for a permission to reconstruct the prototype for track only and got it. In February 1934 the Army Commission was invited to Pilsen to view the three mock-ups of the proposed Škoda SU tank. The first was to have a 66 mm gun and two machine-guns in the front plate, the second a 37 mm gun in a same configuration and the third a 37 mm gun and a machine-gun in a fully rotating turret and another machine-gun in the front plate. The first two mock-ups were actually assault guns, according to World War 2 nomenclature, and though the commission liked certain features of their design, it did not approve them. A prototype of the SU tank was actually built and tested by the Army, but was never accepted for production as Škoda were already working on a new design.

In October 1934 another commission viewed the mock-up of Škoda's new tank, the S-II-a. An order was placed for two prototypes. The construction and the manufacture of the two prototypes took only eight months, certainly a very short time for such an undertaking, and especially by a company which did not have much previous experience with tank manufacture. The Army tests were started in June 1935 and showed the haste with which the construction was finished. There were numerous small and several bigger defects which had to be repaired during the tests. But the influence of Škoda in Army circles was such, that on the basis of incomplete (and not very favourable) tests, and without waiting for new types from ČKD, the order for 160 tanks of the S-II-a type were signed on 30 October 1935.

The first five production tanks, designated LT vz 35, were tested in July 1936 and so many defects were found that the Army returned them for factory repairs. Besides, from January to November 1936, a total of 103 constructional changes were made. This naturally slowed down production.

ABOVE: An S-II-a upgunned with the A-7 3.7 mm Škoda gun as carried by the TNHP-S. It was more effective than the original 3.7 mm vz 34 gun of the LT vz 35 tanks, but only tests were completed.

The design of the LT vz 35 was very modern with adequate armour, armament and communications facilities. There were some progressive features, like pneumatic gear changing and braking. At the same time, it was unproven and very complicated, which caused numerous breakdowns and called for a very high level of driver training. Two more long-term tests were made by the Army in 1937 and again it was found that the LT vz 35 tanks were capable of running only about 2000 km before serious repairs had to be made. But the prestige of Škoda was such that an additional 138 tanks were ordered in 1937.

By continual reconstructions performed even after the tanks were delivered to the Army, they were brought to the standards of a successful fighting vehicle. This was clearly shown during the initial campaigns of World War 2, when they fought with the German and the Romanian armies with considerable success.

The rearmament programme of the Czech Army allowed sufficient funds to order more tanks in 1937. But now the animosity towards the LT vz 35 tanks in the technical branches of the Army was running so high that no more tanks of this type were ordered. Instead, a special group was formed within the Armoured Corps with the task of testing exhaustively all new designs. New orders were to be placed only after the results of these tests were known.

ABOVE: ČKD's prototype LT vz 38 as it looked during the Army trials. Carrying a Skoda A 7 37 mm tank gun and two heavy ZB vz 37 machine-guns, it had maximum armour of 25 mm and a crew of three. The front plate was staggered, both machine-guns were in ball mounts and on the left front side was the base for whip aerial with the combat bar aerial visible on the mudguard behind it. These photographs were actually taken during the demonstration in England in March 1939.

Škoda offered two reconstructed tanks, the S-II-a and S-II-b. ČKD offered a reconstructed LT vz 34 with the engine and drive-train from the TNH tank, the LTL tank, manufactured for the Latvian Army, and the TNHP-S tank, which had been produced already for export. In addition, they presented their new medium tank, V-8-H.

In the tests, both the reconstructed Škoda S-II vehicles were judged inferior to the more modern TNH P-S tank, as they were heavier, had lower speed and shorter endurance and were still not devoid of serious defects.

The reconstructed LT vz 34 tank was found to be highly improved and identical reconstruction was recommended for the remaining 49 tanks already in Army service. The TNH P-S tank was judged vastly superior to all competitors. During a successful three and a half month test it logged 5,584 km, of which 1,954 km were in heavy terrain, without a single serious defect. Its upkeep was easy and did not require more than thirty minutes per day. Similar good results were obtained with the V-8-H medium. It covered, in four months, 4,555 km, of which 1,533 km were in heavy terrain. The incidence of defects was higher than with the TNH type, but acceptable for this much more complicated construction.

Based on the results of these tests, the decision to adopt the TNH P-S as a standard light tank of the Army, the LT vz 38, was made on 1 July, 1938. The V-8-H was accepted as the ST vz 39. 150 LT vz 38 and 300 ST vz 38 were ordered on July 22 1938.

The first twenty LT vz 38 were to be delivered to the 4th Armoured Corps Regiment before the end of 1938. The first ST vz 39 was not expected to be delivered until 1939 due to the longer introduction and development time required. In addition, preparations for manufacture were more complex as it

BELOW: ST vz 39 with a ČKD factory crew during the 1938 Army trials.

had been agreed that Škoda would build about 200 of the ST vz 39 tanks so as to utilize its existing production lines.

None of these vehicles were delivered to the Army, owing to the German occupation of Czechoslovakia in March, 1939.

The total AFV strength of the Czechoslovak Army in March 1939 was 418 tanks and 75 armoured cars. Besides these vehicles on the active list, the Army had 14 experimental tracked vehicles, either prototypes of various series, or modifications which had not been accepted. The complete breakdown of these vehicles is in Table 2.

All these vehicles were seized by the Germans, save the vehicles of the 3rd 'Fast Division', which was stationed in Slovakia. In all, the Slovaks were left with 79 LT vz 35 tanks, 13 OA vz 30 and 30 Tancik vz 33, which were serving in Infantry Divisions in their recce units.

Table 2: AFVs on the Czech Army List – 1939

Type	Designation	Number Held
Armoured car	OA vz 27	24
Armoured car	OA vz 30	51
Tankette	Carden-Loyd	1
Tankette	Tancik vz 33	70
Light tank	Renault	1
Prototype of LT 34	P-II	1
Light tank	LT vz 34	49
Prototype of LT vz 35	S-II-a	1
Light tank	LT vz 35	297
Uparmoured LT vz 34	P-II-b	1
Uparmoured LT vz 35	S-II-b	1
Medium tank	S-III	2
Medium tank	S-II-c	2
Medium tank ST vz 39	V-8-H	2
Prototype of LT vz 38	TNHP-S	2
Joint Venture	SP-II-b	1
Amphibious tank (ČKD)	F-IV-H	1
Amphibious tank (Škoda)	–	1
Anti-tank gun carrier	LKMVP	1

BELOW: ČKD's Amphibious tankette prototype from 1939.

5. Weapons used in the Czechoslovak AFVs

Machine-Guns

Schwarzlose heavy machine-guns, adapted for Mauser 7.92 mm ammunition were used in armoured cars PA-I, PA-II and PA-III. These were manufactured in Czechoslovakia under the designation vz 24 from 1928. Before that, the old war-time Schwarzlose machine-guns were repaired and re-chambered for Mauser ammunition and designated vz 7/24. These water cooled machine-guns were not totally suitable for the use in AFVs, as a puncture of the cooling jacket led to the elimination of the gun. They also used fabric ammunition belts which had some inherent disadvantages of their own.

Česka Zbrojovka Brno began developing heavy machine-guns in 1930 for aircraft use, and side-by-side for use in AFVs. Their aircraft machine-gun ČZ vz 30, though exported actually for use in tanks, was rejected by the Army. At this time the factory already had a new type, ZB 52. This was air-cooled and with a double rate of fire. In 1933 an improved type, ZB 53, was developed and manufactured after extensive trials since 1934. Though the new machine-gun was developed for the use in AFVs, it was used extensively in the fortifications built on the Czechoslovak border from 1935. Under the designation vz 35 the ZB 53 machine-gun was manufactured up to 1936, when an improved version was introduced and designated vz 37.

The ZB machine-guns vz 35 and vz 37 again had a calibre of 7.92 mm and were used in all Czech tanks.

In 1937 a licence for this gun was sold to the BSA factory in Birmingham, England, who manufactured it under the name BESA as a tank machine-gun throughout World War 2.

A third type of machine-gun, used in the Tančik vz 33 and in the armoured car OA vz 30, was the ZB vz 26. It was a very modern and effective weapon. Over 100,000 of these guns were exported from 1926 to 1941 to 21 countries. These guns were exported to Britain beginning in 1930, and from the experience with their use there a new type, ZBG 33, was developed. In May 1935, a licencing agreement with the British War Office was signed and these guns were manufactured as BREN (BRno-ENfield) guns.

ABOVE: The ZB 53 7.92 mm machine-gun in the tank mounting. The Czech Army designation for this was the vz 35 and the later improved model was the vz 37.

BELOW: The portable version of the ZB vz 26 light machine-gun, which was the armament of the Tančik vz 33 and the armoured car OA vz 30. (T. Gander).

Tank Guns

The Škoda anti-tank gun type A-3 was introduced in 1934 as the first specialized anti-tank gun of the Army. It was semi-automatic, with a shell weight of 0.85 kg and muzzle velocity of 675 m/sec. It also fulfilled the main condition: it was effective against 30 mm thick armour of that time up to 1000 m. It was introduced into service as anti-tank gun vz 34.

As early as 1935 it was found that this gun was effective against the improved 30 mm armour only up to 550 m. Therefore the Army asked urgently for a gun with an improved effectiveness. Škoda presented a new gun, type A-4 for trials in 1936. It had the same type of ammunition as the vz

40

ABOVE: A close up view of the two gun mountings in the turret of an LT vz 35 tank. The main armament was the 37 mm vz 34 anti-tank gun (Škoda A-3) with an armoured cowl for the recoil cylinder. Alongside is the separate ball mounted 7.92 mm machine-gun vz 35 which was un-armoured on the LT vz 35. The completely separate ball-mounted machine-gun in the turret of Czechoslovak tanks was a particular feature — German tanks for example, always had the machine-guns co-axial with the main gun. This photograph show a non-running LT vz 35 tank dug in as a fixed fortification.

BELOW: The 37 mm tank gun (Škoda A-7) used in the LT vz 38 and LT vz 40. The German designation for this gun, which was the main armament of the PzKpfw 38(t), was 3.7 cm KwK 37(t).

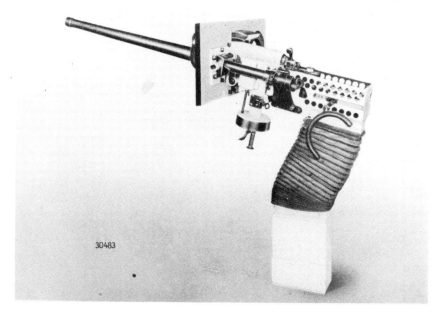

30483

ABOVE: Close up of the breech of a 3.7 cm KwK 37(t) taken from a captured PzKpfw 38(t).

34 with a difference in the powder charge only. The new gun, designated anti-tank gun vz 37, had a muzzle velocity of 750 m/sec. and was effective against the best 32 mm armour up to 1100 m.

The LT vz 34 and LT vz 35 tanks were armed with the anti-tank gun vz 34. Because this was not effective enough, and because it was an adapted field version, not totally suitable for tank use, Škoda was asked to develop a special tank gun for the LT vz 38. Their A-7 type was as effective as the anti-tank gun vz 37, but was adapted specifically for turret use. It was adopted in 1938 as a tank gun vz 38.

The bigger Škoda tank gun type A-9, vz 38, had a calibre of 47 mm. It was adapted for tank use in 1938 and was envisaged for the medium tanks V-8-H and S-II-c. The type A-UV was similar but was for the S-III and S-II-b tanks. Later the anti-tank gun, 47 mm, vz 38 (Škoda A-5), was extensively used by the Germans, as the 4.7 cm PaK (t), being not only used as a wheeled anti-tank gun but also as the main armament of two Panzerjäger vehicles. These were the 4.7 cm PaK (t) (Sfl) auf PzKpfw I Ausf B (Sd Kfz 101) and 4.7 cm PaK (t) auf Pz Kpfw 35 R (f) ohne turm. In 1941 the 4.7 cm KwK 41 (t) (Škoda A-11) was developed but was not accepted for service. The parameters of the Škoda anti-tank and tank guns are summarized in Table III.

Table 3: Škoda Tank Guns

Designation	Tk vz 34	Tk vz 37*	Tk vz 38	PÚV vz 38
Type	A-3	A-7	A-9	A-5
calibre (mm)	37.2	37.2	47.0	47.0
length of barrel (cal)	40.0	47.8	33.7	43.4
muzzle velocity (m/sec)	675.0	750.0	600.0	775.0
weight of shell (kg)	0.85	0.85	1.65	1.65
muzzle energy (mt)	19.8	24.4		50.5
distance effective against 32 mm armour (m)	550.0	1100.0		1500.0

*Škoda anti-tank gun vz 37 (A-4), similar to Škoda tank gun Tk vz 38 (A-7)

Weapons Tests carried out by the German Waffen Prüf 1 on Škoda Guns

Weapon: 3.7 cm PaK 34(t) (Škoda A-3) and 3.7 cm KwK 34(t)
Ammunition: 3.7 cm Pzgr(t) umg
Projectile weight: 0.815 Kg
Muzzle velocity: 690 m·sec

Range in meters	Penetration at 30°
100	37.0 mm
200	35.5 mm
300	34.1 mm
400	32.6 mm
500	31.3 mm
600	30.1 mm
700	28.9 mm
800	27.8 mm
900	26.7 mm
1000	25.7 mm
1100	24.9 mm
1200	24.1 mm
1300	23.3 mm
1400	22.8 mm
1500	22.3 mm

Weapon: 3.7 cm PaK 37(t) (Škoda A-4) and 3.7 cm KwK 38(t) (Škoda A-7)
Ammunition: 3.7 cm Pzgr (t) umg   3.7 cm Pzgr 40
Projectile Weight: 0.815 Kg   0.368 Kg
Muzzle velocity: 750 m·sec   1040 m·sec

Penetration at 30°	Penetration at 30°
40.5 mm	64.0 mm
39.0 mm	53.0 mm
37.6 mm	45.0 mm
36.2 mm	38.0 mm
34.8 mm	
33.6 mm	
32.3 mm	
31.0 mm	
29.8 mm	
28.7 mm	
27.6 mm	
26.6 mm	
25.6 mm	
24.8 mm	
24.0 mm	

Weapon: 4.7 cm PaK 38(t) (Škoda A-5). The 1941 experimental 4.7 cm KwK 41(t) (Škoda A-11) had similar performance.

Ammunition:	4.7 cm Pzgr (ö) umg	4.7 cm Pzgr 36(t)	4.7 cm Pzgr
Projectile weight:	1.51 kg	1.65 kg	0.825 kg
Muzzle velocity:	805 m·sec	782 m·sec	1080 m·sec
Range in metres	**Penetration at 30°**	**Penetration at 30°**	**Penetration at 30°**
100	44.0 mm	53.5 mm	99.5 mm
200	43.4 mm	52.0 mm	87.0 mm
300	42.8 mm	50.5 mm	76.0 mm
400	42.0 mm	49.0 mm	67.0 mm
500	41.1 mm	47.7 mm	59.0 mm
600	39.9 mm	46.3 mm	51.6 mm
700	38.6 mm	44.9 mm	45.0 mm
800	37.2 mm	43.5 mm	38.6 mm
900	35.6 mm	42.0 mm	
1000	34.0 mm	40.7 mm	
1100	32.3 mm	39.5 mm	
1200	30.5 mm	38.1 mm	
1300	28.7 mm	37.0 mm	
1400	27.0 mm	35.6 mm	
1500	24.9 mm	34.5 mm	

BELOW: By May 1941 351 fixed fortifications, mounting the turret of the PzKpfw 38(t) had been built. The standard turret and armament was used. These turrets were available as a result of the factory conversion of tanks to self propelled guns and recce vehicles. In all there were 435 such turrets available, taken from the unfinished PzKpfw 38(t) Ausf G converted to carry the 7.62 cm PaK 36(r), refurbished tank chassis used to make 7.5 cm PaK 40 conversions in 1943 and also those taken from tanks converted to the Aufklärungspanzer 38(t) in 1944.

6. Pre-war Exports of AFVs

CZECHOSLOVAK factories were actively exporting arms and munitions to the Balkan countries between the two wars. It was only natural, therefore, that as soon as they had AFVs to offer, they did so. In June 1933 ČKD asked the Ministry of Defence for an approval to export tanks to Romania. As this particular model, a two man light tank or tankette, was not used by the Czechoslovak Army (AH-IV), they got the necessary approval. At the same time, both ČKD and Škoda were demonstrating the developments of their tankettes in Yugoslavia in July 1933. Škoda influence prevailed and Yugoslavia ordered eight vehicles of the T-3D type, a heavy version of the earlier Škoda tankettes, armed with a 37 mm gun. Škoda delivered these vehicles in 1938.

ČKD started actively exporting their AH-IV series tanks in 1935. The first 50 vehicles of this type were delivered to Iran in 1935-6 where they

BELOW: The T-3-D tankettes of the Yugoslav army on the move. Called T-32 in Yugoslavian service, it carried the very effective 37 mm Škoda gun and had frontal armour of 30 mm. Eight vehicles were delivered in 1938.

ABOVE: The AH-IV tankette already in Iranian markings during factory trials. These vehicles were delivered in a tropicalized version, known as 'RH' in Iran.

were known as the 'RH', then followed Romania with an order for 35 vehicles, designated R-1, in 1936 and finally Sweden bought 48 vehicles, AH-IV Sv, in 1937-8. The less developed countries usually bought complete vehicles, while countries like Sweden (and later Switzerland) specified their own engines and armaments.

The AH-IV light tank was ordered even after the war. In 1950 Ethiopia was looking for a light tank, armed with machine-guns only, easy to maintain and rugged enough for the rock and desert terrain of Ethiopia.

BELOW: The Romanian AH-IV was designated R-1. These vehicles were comparable in armour and armament to PzKpfw I. This is the commander's model fitted with the observation cupola on the turret.

ABOVE: The AH-IV-Sv was designated Stvr m/37 in Sweden. At 4.8 tons it was the heaviest of the series, but the more powerful Scania-Vabis engine gave it comparable performance. Armour was again 15 mm, but both 8 mm Ksp M/39 machine-guns were in the turret, which carried a small cupola for the commander. Here the prototype is being tested by a Swedish delegation to ČKD in November 1937. (D. von Porat).

A Swedish Colonel Salin, who was at that time a military advisor to the Emperor, was familiar with the ČKD tanks used in the Swedish Army, and he proposed the AH-IV tank. As the Ethiopian Army asked for an air-cooled engine, ČKD modified the tank by using the Tatra 111 air-cooled diesel engine, proven during the war in German armoured cars and heavy trucks. The tanks were delivered and the training of the Ethiopian crews was supervised by Czech experts. These light tanks were a great success despite their 20-year-old design.

Skoda sold 126 of their S-II-a tanks to Romania in 1936. (In Romania they were designated R-2) and was trying to sell them to the Soviet Union and Britain as well. Afghanistan ordered ten tanks in 1938. These were manufactured as T-11, and supplied in the Summer of 1940 to Bulgaria.

ČKD in the meantime was busily exporting their light tank, and the TNH series. The first 50 vehicles of this type were ordered by Iran and delivered between 1935-7 in a tropicalized version. The Iranian Army formed the 1st and 2nd Divisions of the Imperial Iranian Ground Forces, each having 25 of the AH-IV tanks and 25 TNH tanks. These tanks were used up to 1957.

In 1938 Peru bought 24 vehicles of the LTP type. In 1937 Switzerland ordered 24 tanks of the LTH type and specified for them Sauer Aarbon diesel engines and 24 mm Oerlikon guns. Later she negotiated a licence for manufacturing the LTH tanks. After the war 158 of the Hetzer tank hunter were purchased.

In 1937 Sweden ordered, through Jungner Co., 48 AH-IV-Sv light tanks,

LEFT: The Ethiopian Army received their AH-IV tankettes in 1950. These were very similar to the R-1 supplied to Romania before the war, however, they were powered by the aircooled diesel motor — Tatra 111.

designated in the Swedish Army as Strv m/37. These had Scania-Vabis engines, Swedish machine-guns, optics and radios. They were assembled in Sweden by Oskarshamms Shipyard. As these were fairly successful, the Swedish Army ordered two prototypes of the TNH-Sv tank, followed by an

BELOW: The TNH tanks ordered by Iran in 1935 were the direct predecessors of the LT vz 38 and PzKpfw 38(t) tanks. Though sporting a turret of a different shape with a cast cupola on the left side, most of the later components were already used on these tanks.

ABOVE: The LTP in Peruvian service. It had frontal armour of 32 mm and was armed with the vz 34 gun.

order for 90 vehicles in 1939. These tanks were never delivered due to the German occupation.

The last export order was placed by Latvia in 1938 for 21 vehicles of the LTL type, armed with an Oerlikon 20 mm gun and two machine-guns. A prototype of this series with an untypical rear drive was manufactured, but the beginning of World War 2 cancelled the delivery. It is probable that the LT vz 40 vehicles sold to the Slovak Army in 1940, were built with the components manufactured for the LTL.

BELOW: LTH weighed 7.5 tons with its 32 mm frontal armour and had a maximum speed of 45 km/hour. In Switzerland the tanks were designated Pz 39.

TOP OF PAGE: In 1943, the Swiss Army developed a prototype for a selfpropelled anti-tank gun, CH (or 'Nahkampfkanone I'), based on the LTH components. The 10 ton vehicle carried the 75 mm gun in a totally enclosed superstructure. Crew was 5 men.

ABOVE: Rear view of the CH, showing the modification to the engine deck.

TOP OF PAGE: Another Swiss prototype for a self-propelled 105 mm howitzer on the modified LTH chassis. A longer superstructure was needed to accommodate the larger gun.

ABOVE: A prototype of the LTL tank, developed for Latvia in 1938. This was the only ČKD tank with the rear drive. It was armed with a 20 mm Oerlikon gun.

7. Czechoslovak Fully Tracked Artillery Tractors

DURING World War 1 the emphasis had been on artillery tractors which had large diameter wheels. The Czechoslovak Army was initially equipped with artillery tractors of this type, namely the Škoda U and later the Škoda Z which had been designed by Praga, but were built by Škoda. 152 such vehicles were held by the Army. In 1925 the German Hanomag WD 25 PS and WD 50 PS fully tracked tractors were tested alongside prototypes of the Tatra-Škoda KH 50 wheel-cum-track vehicle. As a result Breitfeld-Daněk, later part of ČKD, received an order to build a number of the 25PS tractors under licence from Hanomag.

The Tatra-Škoda KH 50 had been designed from 1924 by Vollmer, and was being offered both as an armoured vehicle and as an artillery tractor. A number of countries purchased examples of the rear engined wheel-cum-track vehicle. In 1928 a 60 HP engine was fitted and the designation changed to KH 60 and 1930 saw the KH 70 with a 70 HP motor.

Starting in 1930 Škoda attempted to provide fully tracked artillery tractors of all sizes for the Army and export. The lightest was also the most successful. This was the Škoda MTH, 54 of which were ordered by the Army in 1935 and were delivered up to 1939. This was a 36 HP vehicle driving rear sprockets and it had running gear based on the suspension of the MUV tankettes. For the medium tractor Škoda offered the STH. This 4.6 ton vehicle was a less sophisticated caterpillar tractor powered by a 45 HP engine (4 cylinder water-cooled, 4850 cc). It only had a speed of 14.2 Km/hr and a range of 61 Km. It was supposed to tow 150 mm guns. The Army were not too interested and Škoda attempted to improve performance with a 66 HP SHD diesel motor and a 60 HP 5,530 cc version of the SH engine, speed was now 21 Km/hr. A similar tractor the VTH was supposed to fulfill the task of towing heavy guns, but it was not adopted by the Army.

Learning from their experience in the KH project with Škoda, Tatra developed a heavy artillery tractor also with the wheel-cum-track suspension. However, the change from wheels to tracks and back again was controlled by hydraulics from the driving cab. The designation of this tractor was Tatra KTT and it was powered by a 6 cylinder water-cooled engine developing 120 HP. By the time this KTT tractor was available the interest in wheel-cum-tracks had waned. Tatra next offered, in 1937, a medium tractor V 740. This vehicle was competing for the Army orders against the

ABOVE: The so-called gun truck vz 24 Škoda Martin 540 is seen here transporting a Breitfeld-Daněk tractor complete with field gun and crew. The Breitfeld-Daněk tractos were licensed versions of the German Hanomag WD 25 PS.

ČKD T IV. The V740 had a 65 HP watercooled engine of 7,480 cc. In the end no orders were placed.

During the mid thirties ČKD had been very active in seeking orders for their military products. In addition to the range of tanks they developed a range of artillery tractors which were offered for export. In 1937 the Army ordered 25 Praga T IV from ČKD as a medium artillery tractor. This vehicle used running gear based on the earlier prototypes of the V-8-H tank. The engine was a 56 HP 4 cylinder water-cooled unit. The T IV could tow a 4 ton load, carry 1 ton and it was fitted with a winch to pull 5 tons. A crew of 6 men could be carried. Also in 1937 ČKD secured their first export orders for the most successful artillery tractor in their range, the T VI. In various forms the T VI was built until 1944 and it was exported to several countries. In 1937

BELOW: Tatra KTT wheel-cum-track artillery tractor was an offshoot of the 'Kolohousenka' series. On this vehicle the change was made hydraulically from the driver's seat.

ABOVE: T VI-T awaiting delivery to Turkey in the yard of the ČKD works in Prague.

Romania ordered the T VI-R and in 1938 orders were received from Turkey for the T VI-T. Portugal ordered the T VI-P. These tractors had a truck type cab and body to carry the crew and ammunition load. The engine was a 75 HP 6 cylinder water-cooled 7,800 cc engine.

A more powerful version of the T VI appeared when Sweden ordered the T VI-Sv. This was fitted with the Praga AE motor which was similar to that which was to be used in the TNH-Sv tanks which Sweden was interested in purchasing from ČKD. The AE engine was a 6 cylinder water-cooled OHV of 7,750 cc and it developed 90 HP at 1800 rpm. A five speed gearbox was used. Production of the T VI continued at BMM after the German occupation and most of the T VI tractors were exported to the German Allies. One report indicates that Romania received 221 T VI R-P tractors in 1942. These had the more powerful AE motor and can be identified by the 19 air louvres in the engine side covers, in place of the more common 7 flaps which could be opened or closed. On some of these Romanian vehicles the rubber tyred road wheels were replaced by steel rimmed wheels.

In September 1942 the Waffen-SS ordered 500 T VI-SS tractors from BMM and in January 1942 some T VI R-P from the Romanian order were used in comparison trials with the RSO. The Slovak army purchased 30 T VI tractors from the total of 188 tractors of all types manufactured by BMM in 1943. The production for the Waffen-SS order was slow to get underway and by February 1944 only 16 T VI-SS had been completed, at that time there were 120 in production and parts and materials for another 200 available. However, by the time production was suspended only 73 T VI-SS had been delivered. The T VI-SS can be identified by the all steel wheels and the German trailer indicator on the driver cab roof.

Back in 1938 ČKD also developed a light tractor the T III. The suspension and running gear were based on that of the AH-IV tankettes. The engine was a 6 cylinder water-cooled 4,300 cc unit which developed 77 HP. The T

ABOVE: Büssing -NAG designed the sWs but this was then manufactured by Tatra. In 1953 Tatra produced the T 809 which was essentially the sWs modernised and powered by a Tatra V 12 cylinder air-cooled diesel engine.

III could tow 1.8 tons. Designated 'leichter Raupenschlepper T-3-III', 126 were built by BMM for the German Army. Also in 1938 ČKD had developed the T V tractor especially for the Dutch East Indies Army. It had a conventional truck cab and a flat bed load platform. The suspension and running gear were in this case based on the successful LT export tank series. The T V tractors had a 90 HP version of the 6 cylinder 7,750 cc engine, and a five speed gearbox. It appears that these T V tractors were confiscated and used by the Germans after the occupation.

The T VII was also developed in 1938 and had a 112 HP 6 cylinder water-cooled TO engine of 11,530 cc. The heaviest of the ČKD tractors was the T IX which was designed to tow up to 15 tons. Powered by a V 8 Cylinder engine of 14,230 cc which developed 140 HP it was immediately adopted by the Germans in 1939. Production of the 'schwerer Raupenschlepper T-9' continued until 1943 during which time 76 had been delivered.

During the war Škoda built the German 3t Zgkw semi-track tractor and also the ill fated Porsche Rad Schlepper Ost, which returned to the large diameter wheel design.

Tatra co-operated with the development of the sWS (Schwerer Wehrmachtschlepper) and built some of these vehicles in 1944 and 1945.

8. Wartime Use of AFVs

SLOVAKIA declared itself an autonomous state on 14 March, 1939 and the next day, Germany began the occupation of Bohemia and Moravia and included them in the Third Reich as a Protectorate. The Czechoslovak Army was disbanded and all its equipment and weapons were confiscated. All the tanks were transported to the Dresden area, where they were overhauled and equipped with German radio sets, optics and tools.

As has already been mentioned, ČKD won the Czech Army trials with their LT vz 38 and obtained an order for 150 vehicles to be delivered before May 1939. But, because all the special emergency appropriations were revoked after the Munich agreement, production was so slowed down that the first vehicles were not ready until 22 May, 1939. The Germans duly took over the first nine tanks and tested them. They were impressed, as the LT vz 38 was vastly superior to their own PzKpfw I and II both in armour and firepower and was as good as the current versions of the PzKpfw III.

Therefore, ČKD (renamed Böhmisch-Mährische Maschinenfabrik under the new German directorship) was ordered to step up production and finish the 150 ordered vehicles as soon as possible. In June 1939, three further orders for 325 tanks, now renamed PzKpfw 38 (t) (for *tschech* or *Czech* in German), were placed.

From May to August 1939, BMM delivered 78 PzKpfw 38 (t) Ausf A. At that time of Operation *Fall Weiss*, or the invasion of Poland, two of the six participating German panzer divisions, the 1st and 3rd Leichte Divisions had four tank battalions equipped with Czech tanks. Of the 112 PzKpfw 35 (t) and 59 PzKpfw 38 (t) used, 77 and 7 respectively were damaged, but most were later repaired. In January 1940 the Germans endorsed the success of the PzKpfw 38 (t) and another 275 were ordered.

Fifteen PzKpfw 38 (t) took part in the occupation of Norway, code named *Wesserübung Nord*, but were brought back quickly to take part in the attack on France, or *Fall Gelb*. After Poland the Germans upgraded some of their Leichte Divisions to full Panzer Divisions so that of the ten participating Panzer Divisions, three were equipped with Czech tanks. The 6th Panzer Division had all the PzKpfw 35 (t), while the 7th and 8th were equipped with the PzKpfw 38(t). 357 Czech tanks participated, 229 of these being the PzKpfw 38(t). During this campaign 54 PzKpfw 38(t) were damaged and six subsequently scrapped.

The Germans turned East for their next target, and invaded the Balkans in

ABOVE: This PzKpfw 38(t) Ausf B or C carries the old type of smoke generators on the right rear mud-guard next to the jerry-can. Russia, Summer 1941. (Bundesarchiv).

early 1941. Code named *Unternehmen 25*, the occupation of Yugoslavia and Greece was spearheaded by six Panzer Divisions. The 8th Panzer Division still had its 125 PzKpfw 38(t).

In June 1941 seventeen Panzer Divisions took part in the initial stages of *Unternehmen Barbarossa*, the attack on the Soviet Union. Six of these, more than one third of the Panzer Divisions employed, mustered a total of 160 PzKpfw 35(t) and 674 PzKpfw 38(t). Moreover, the Romanian 1st Royal Armoured Division was equipped with the R-2 tanks, and their 1st Cavalry Division had the R-1. The Slovak 'Fast Division' was equipped with a mixture of LT vz 35, LT vz 38 and LT vz 40. The Czech tanks represented more than one quarter of the total strength of the German Panzer formations. The fighting was much harder in Russia and the opposing tanks of a different quality. In the first six months of the conflict, the German Army lost 796 PzKpfw 38(t) alone.

By early 1942 it was clear that lightly armoured tanks with small calibre guns were no longer acceptable as the primary main battle tanks. The Germans started passing new and refurbished ones to their Allies the Romanians, Hungarians and Slovaks to bolster their tank formations. Production in BMM was changed over to tank destroyers and self-propelled guns. Even so, there were still 229 PzKpfw 38(t) tanks on the active list as late as September 1944. By then they were used mostly in anti-partisan and policing duties and as parts of armoured trains.

BMM manufactured the basic tank up to June 1942, while the first modification, the Panzerjäger 38(t) with a 7.62 cm PaK 36(r) was produced from April 1942. In all, sixteen modifications were developed and manufactured in great numbers up to April 1945.

Table 4: German Units equipped with Czech Tanks

Fall Weiss (Poland 1939)
1st Leichte Division
6th Panzer Brigade
    Panzer Regiment 11
    Panzer Abeilung 65   112 PzKpfw 35(t)

3rd Leichte Division
    Panzer Abeilung 67   59 PzKpfw 38(t)

Weserübung Nord (Norway 1940)
XXXI Armee Korps
3rd Panzer Züge   15 PzKpfw 38(t)

Fall Gelb (France 1940)
6th Panzer Division
    Panzer Regiment 11
    Panzer Abeilung 65   118 PzKpfw 35(t), 10 PzBefW 35(t)

7th Panzer Division
    Panzer Regiment 25   106 PzKpfw 38(t)

8th Panzer Division
    Panzer Regiment 10
    Panzer Abteilung 67   116 PzKpfw 38(t), 7 PzBefW 38(t)

Unternehmen 25 (Yugoslavia, Greece 1941)
8th Panzer Division
    Panzer Regiment 10   118 PzKpfw 38(t), 7 PzBefW 38(t)

Unternehmen Barbarossa (Soviet Union 1941)
6th Panzer Division
    Panzer Regiment 11
    Panzer Abteilung 65   149 PzKpfw 35(t), 11 PzBefW 35(t)

7th Panzer Division
    Panzer Regiment 25   167 PzKpfw 38(t), 7 PzBefW 38(t)

8th Panzer Division
    Panzer Regiment 10   118 PzKpfw 38(t), 7 PzBefW 38(t)

12th Panzer Division
    Panzer Regiment 29   107 PzKpfw 38(t), 10 PzBefw 38(t)

19th Panzer Division
    Panzer Regiment 27   118 PzKpfw 38(t), 7 PzBefW 38(t)

20th Panzer Division
    Panzer Regiment 21   113 PzKpfw 38(t), 10 PzBefW 38(t)

ABOVE: An alternative version of the Befehlspanzer 38(t) being prepared for the Victory celebration in Paris after its capture in 1940. Instead of the frame antenna this tank has an additional German 2 meter rod on the mud-guard. The original Czech aerial is still used. (Bundesarchiv).

In April 1944, the Jagdpanzer Hetzer started rolling off the assembly lines at BMM and in September at Škoda. In all, 6,450 vehicles based on the 38(t) chassis were manufactured by both BMM and Škoda.

In October 1944 the decision was made in Germany to base all new AFV constructions on two chassis solely, the Panther and the 38(t) or (d), while the production of all other German tank chassis was to be discontinued. The simplicity, ruggedness, ease of manufacture and maintenance of the original ČKD construction was paid the highest accolade by the Germans, against whom it was originally developed.

BELOW: LT vz 35 Skoda tanks were renamed PzKpfw 35(t) and used by the Wehrmacht in Poland, France and Russian campaigns. The tank on the left is a Befehlswagen (command vehicle) with additional radio equipment and a frame antenna. (Bundesarchiv)

9. Wartime Exports of AFVs

EXPORTS during the war years were naturally limited to Germany's allies, who were fighting side-by-side with them and did not have enough facilities to produce their own tanks.

Romania

Romania bought, in the late thirties, two types of Czech tanks, the R-1 tankette (ČKD's AH-IV) and the R-2 light tank, (Škoda's S-II-a or LT vz 35). After the reorganization of the Romanian Army under German supervision, all the 126 R-2 tanks were grouped into the 1st Royal Armoured Division, while the R-1 tankettes were retained by the élite 1st Royal Cavalry Division.

Both units were very active during the drive to Odessa and during its siege. The 1st Royal Armoured Division at the time of Stalingrad still had about 100 R-2 tanks, supported by a small number of German PzKpfw III and IV, on its rolls. The losses at Stalingrad were so heavy that in March 1943 the

BELOW: R-2 of the 1st Royal Romanian Armoured Division on Don, November 1942. Note the National insignia on the glacis plate. (Bundesarchiv).

ABOVE: Late war Romanian conversion was mounting the Russian 7.62 cm gun on the R-2 chassis.

Division had to be replenished with 50 PzKpfw 38(t) from German stocks. The R-2 tanks which did not succumb to the Russian onslaught were soon withdrawn from front line service and some were converted to a self-propelled gun by mounting the captured Russian M42 7.62 cm gun in an open top superstructure. Some of these tanks and a few of the R-1 were still in service with the Romanian Army until 1955. The Romanians tried unsuccessfully to order 200 T-21 from Škoda in 1940.

Slovakia

The infant Slovak Army inherited 79 LT vz 35 tanks from the 3rd 'Fast Division' of the Czechoslovak Army. Two of these tanks were lost almost immediately during a border incident with Hungary. As this number was not sufficient for equipping a Slovak 'Fast Division', the Slovak Army bought 32 PzKpfw 38(t) tanks from the Germans and ordered another 21 tanks of the LT vz 40 type directly from BMM. The LT vz 40 was a lighter and cheaper version of the PzKpfw 38(t) similar to the pre-war tanks exported to Switzerland and Peru. Evidence suggests that the LT vz 40 was probably based on Latvian LTL tanks, whose manufacture got under way in late 1938, but which were not delivered. The LT vz 40, however, carried the same armament and had the same engine as the PzKpfw 38(t), but was lighter, with a different shape turret with a small cast cupola integrated in the escape hatch and only two return rollers. The Slovak Army had mostly gun tanks and at least two command tanks with the original LT turret in late 1940.

At the time of the attack on the Soviet Union in July 1941, the Slovak

ABOVE: One of the few remaining mobile LT vz 35 tanks of the Slovak Army during the Slovak National uprising, August 1944.

BELOW: Some LT vz 35 tanks which were no longer capable of moving on their own were incorporated as parts of the three armoured trains the Slovak insurgents built. The tanks were placed on flat cars and encased in an armoured superstructure so that only their turrets showed.

ABOVE: During the National Slovak uprising the ČKD tanks fought for the first time against the Germans. But in 1944 it was too late and they were no match against Hetzer, PzKpfw IV, Panthers and even Tigers. This is an Ausf E or F with the National shield on the turret.

'Fast Division' had a complement of 114 tanks in a tank Regiment, whose first battalion was equipped with the LT vz 35 and the other with LT vz 38 and LT vz 40. The 'Fast Division' was fighting as part of the Armee Gruppe Sud and participated in the drive to Caucasus. But after the Stalingrad battle it had to retreat and lost most of its heavy equipment during early 1943.

During 1943 and even into 1944 some of these losses were made up by the delivery of 37 more PzKpfw 38(t) and some German PzKpfw II and III. In April 1944 the Slovaks received a futher Czech vehicle, the self-propelled anti-tank gun 7.5 cm PaK 40/3 Auf PzKpfw 38(t) Ausf H (Sd Kfz 138), a total of 18 were delivered.

The Slovak Army maintained some tank units in the homeland, and at the time of the National Uprising in August 1944 had 30 LT vz 38, several LT vz 40 and LT vz 35 on hand. This was the first time that the Czech tanks were fighting against the Germans, but in 1944 they were hopelessly outclassed by the 7.5 cm and 8.8 cm guns of the more modern German armour.

Bulgaria

Bulgaria got 26 PzKpfw 35(t) from the Germans in February 1940, later she was supplied with PzKpfw 38(t), receiving 10 of them in early 1943. Directly from Škoda Bulgaria purchased 10 T-11 (PzKpfw 35(t)) that had been built for Afghanistan. These were delivered in mid-1940.

ABOVE: Probably the last surviving PzKpfw 28(t) in running condition is today preserved as a memorial to the Slovak National Uprising of 1944 in Banska Bystrica, Slovakia. It is an early model having the staggered 25 mm drivers' plate of the Ausf A to C. The czech flag and numbers were added after the war.

Hungary

Hungary manufactured tanks of her own before the war, namely the Toldi light tank and the Nimrod self-propelled gun, based on the Landswerk licence obtained from Sweden. In 1939 it was decided to manufacture a medium tank and an approach was made to the Germans in an attempt to obtain a licence for manufacturing the PzKpfw III. As the Germans were not willing to grant this licence at that time, they recommended the Škoda medium tank, the S-II-c.

This had not been finished for the Czechoslovak Army trials in 1938, but renamed T-21, it was futher developed and improved. This resulted in the T-22 medium, which was shown to the Honved comission in Pilsen in May 1940 and was again demonstrated in Hungary during June and July 1940. The licencing agreement for the T-22 tank was signed in August 1940, followed in November 1940 by a licencing agreement for the Škoda gun model A-17. This was an adaption of the A-7 tank gun to 4 cm calibre, capable of using the ammunition Hungary was already manufacturing for its Nimrod 4 cm Bofors gun and its 4 cm anti-tank guns.

The T-22 tank was manufactured with only slight modifications in Hungary under the name 40M Turán in two gun variants, Turan I carrying the 4 cm gun and Turán II a 7.5 cm gun. Later on, the Hungarians developed an assault gun on Turán chassis, carrying a 10.5 cm gun, and named it 40/43M Zrinyi.

The total licenced production, according to Škoda sources, was for 300 Turán I, 322 Turán II and 40 Zrinyi assault guns.

ABOVE: The 40M Túran had an improved superstructure with a fewer plates, 50 mm front armour and 25 mm side armour, which was sloped at 10°. Production began in late 1941 and the initial order of 230 tanks was to be completed in 1942. These tanks were used to re-equip the 1st Pancelos Hadosztaly (Panzer Division) after it was reformed in Budapest 1943.

In June 1942 Hungary bought from Germany 102 PzKpfw 38(t) and some German PzKpfw IV, to equip their 1st Pancelos Hadosztaly (Panzer Division). Most of these were lost after the collapse of the Don Front in early 1943. In October and November 1944 Hungary acquired 50 Hetzer tank hunters, followed by another 50 in January and February 1945. These vehicles were employed during the battle for Budapest.

BELOW: A Hungarian Zrinyi assault gun which proved a very successful descendant of the Škoda T-22. The Zrinyi only appeared armed with a 10.5 cm Howitzer. Plans to introduce a Zrinyi armed with the 7.5 cm L/43 gun were interrupted by the German occupation of Hungary in March 1944. Hungarian assault gun units were however, equipped with the German StuG III and later the Hetzer.

ABOVE: A close-up view of the modified turret fitted to the Strv m/41 S-II. The S-II wa slightly longer with a greater gap between the two wheel bogies. On these late production vehicles a new type of two shackle was welded to the nose plate. (Swedish Armour Association).

Sweden

The Defence Act of 1936 envisaged a build-up of Swedish tank forces; proposed to consist of two independent tank battalions. The Swedish Parliament appropriated 4.5 million Swedish Crowns for tank procurement, but this sum was not sufficient to buy contemporary light gun tanks, even for one of the planned battalions. Therefore, Sweden bought the 48 AH-IV tankettes from ČKD for assembly in Sweden, designated Strv m/37, and only 16 gun tanks m/38 from Landswerk. The tankettes were all delivered by February 1939 and used mainly for training until better vehicles could be procured. ČKD had, by now, interested the Swedish in their TNH, which had been ordered by the Czech Army as the LT vz 38. They offered Sweden a special version, designated TNH-Sv which could be completed with Swedish equipment and fittings. The German occupation intervened in March 1939.

The outbreak of war stressed the need for speedy organization and equipment of Swedish tank forces. AB Landswerk had orders for 120 vehicles of the improved Strv m/38 model, now designated m/39 and m/40. But at the same time in late 1939, Sweden contacted BMM and ordered 90 tanks of the TNH-Sv type. BMM started tooling for this series, but the German forces in 1940 needed every tank they could get and were not

ABOVE: An Sav m/43 during post war manouveres. The SAV m/43 was redesignated Sav 101 and fitted with a new gun, having its recoil cylinder beneath the barrel. It served until 1970. (Swedish Armour Association).

willing to allow further production for export orders. During 1940 it was decided to confiscate these tanks for use by the Germans. On the other hand, the good will of Sweden was quite important to Germany, and so licencing talks were started and in December 1940 agreement was reached.

In early 1941 Sweden ordered a mild steel prototype with no armament, engine or optics to be prepared, and delivered in April 1941; a Scania Vabis

BELOW: Sav m/43 was an assault gun based on the Strv M/41 S-II chassis. It carried the 105 mm m/44 gun in a totally enclosed superstructure. Weight was 12 tons and max speed 43 km/hr.

ABOVE: Two Swedish self propelled guns based upon the chassis of the Strv m/41 were the PvKv 4, on the right, armed with a 75 mm L/60 anti-aircraft gun and the PvKv 3 with a 57 mm anti-tank gun in the centre. The vehicle on the left is the PvKv 2 which was based on the Landsverk Strv m/40 which also had the 57 mm but in an armoured sleeve. (Swedish Armour Association).

1664 6 cylinder engine to be mounted in the prototype. BMM delivered the prototype to Stockholm in June 1941 and after it was tested, an order was placed with Scania Vabis for 116 tanks, designated Stvr m/41, armed with a Bofors 37 mm gun and Swedish machine-guns.

In June 1942 another 122 tanks were ordered, though only 104 were completed. This improved model was designated Strv m/41 S-II. The engine was the Scania Vabis 603/2 6 cylinder water cooled 8,470 cc developing 160 HP at 2300 rpm which improved the power to weight ratio and performance. The second series tanks also were longer and had a modified turret where the sides of the turret front were sloped rather than vertical. In February 1943 Scania Vabis were ordered to build a prototype assault gun using the Strv m/41 chassis. In fact the prototype was built from the original mild steel tank delivered by BMM in 1941. The prototype Stormartillerivagen m/43

BELOW: PvKv 4 mounting the 75 mm L/60 anti-aircraft gun. (Swedish Armour Association).

ABOVE: A prototype of the Bofors fm 43—45 recoilless 15 cm gun on the Stvr m/41 chassis was built in 1945, but never attained production. (J C Probst).

(Sav m/43) was fitted with a Bofors 75 mm m/02 L/27. Scania Vabis built 18 Sav m/43 but armed with a new 105 mm Sak m/44. Later 18 of Sav m/43 were built on tank chassis from the original S-II order. Photographic evidence shows that the 105 mm Sak m/44 was subsequently replaced by a gun on which the recoil gear was situated below the barrel. While the Strv m/41 tanks were phased out in 1957 the Sav m/43 redesignated as the Sav 101 was in active service until 1970.

BELOW: One of the prototypes for the Swedish Pvb 301 armoured personnel carrier. On production vehicles the machine-gun turret was replaced by a remote controlled 20 mm cannon.

ABOVE: Front and rear views of the Pvb 301. Its performance was much superior to that of the Strv m/41 as about 20 per cent more power was delivered to the tracks by the new 150 hp air cooled diesel engine.

To meet the threat during the Korean war, in the early fifties a small number of the Swedish Strv m/41 tanks were converted to self-propelled guns to prolong the useful life of the chassis. The PvKv 3 mounted the 57 mm anti-tank gun while the PvKv 4 carried the 75 mm L/60 anti-aircraft gun, in a fully traversing open-topped turret.

The Swedish Army still wished to utilize the very reliable chassis and in 1957 a design study indicated that an armoured personnel carrier could be built on the Strv m/41 chassis. Hagglunds were ordered to develop the Pvb 301. A new superstructure, engine and a 20 mm gun mount were developed and from 1960 to 1963 all the Strv m/41 were converted to Pvb 301. The original turrets were installed in bunkers to provide airfield protection.

Towards the end of World War 2, a self-propelled gun prototype was built using the Strv m/41 chassis mounting the new Bofors recoilless 15 cm experimental gun fm/43-45, but this never entered service.

10. Development of the 38 (t) Series During the War

THE LT vz 38 had a combat weight of 9.4 tons and carried a crew of three. It was armed with the Škoda 37 mm A-7 tank gun and two 7.92 mm ZB vz 37 machine-guns. Armour was 25 mm front, 15 mm sides and 10-12 mm on top, riveted. The top of superstructure was bolted.

The suspension consisted of four large rubber-tyred wheels, front driving sprocket, idler and two return rollers. Track was made from manganese nickel steel. The Praga EPA six cylinder overhead valve engine developed 125 HP at 2,200 rpm. This gave the tank maximum speed on road of 48 km/hour and about 20 km/hour in medium terrain. Fuel consumption was roughly 80 litres/100 km on the road, which corresponded to an action radius of 250 km.

The turret had no basket and was traversed by hand. The commander's cupola was fixed and had four periscopes. Both machine-guns were mounted in ball mounts, the hull machine-gun had a provision for firing by the driver by a Bowden cable from one of the steering levers, the turret weapon could be locked with the gun or operated independently. The commander/gunner sighted the gun through a coaxial telescopic sight and moved it either by a shoulder pad or used an elevating gear. The gun was semi-automatic and could fire both armour piercing (AP) and high explosive (HE) shells. Ninety rounds for the gun in spring-loaded magazines and 2,400 rounds for the machine-guns in belts were carried.

The radio was mounted on the left front of the hull and was connected to two aerials, the whip aerial giving range of about 5 km, and the 'combat' bar aerial on the mud guard or fender having a range of only 1 km. The tank had no intercom and the commander communicated with the driver using coloured lights. There were two main exits, one through the cupola hatch and one via the hull gunner's hatch.

As has already been mentioned, ČKD delivered the first nine LT vz 38 vehicles on 22 May, 1939. The Germans tested them, were favourably impressed and decided to have the original order for 150 tanks completed, with minor modifications, for their army. The designation was changed to PzKpfw 38(t).

PzKpfw 38(t) Ausf A was practically identical to LT vz 38 as ordered by the Czechs and was produced from May to November 1939 for the total of 150 vehicles. German radio sets and optics were installed and the usual lavish stowage provided. A fourth crew member, the turret gunner, was added. Circular bolted splash guards were added around the machine-gun ball mounts.

PzKpfw 38(t) Ausf B was manufactured from January to May 1940. It had some small changes in external stowage, Notek lights were installed and some tanks were equipped with smoke projectors on the rear plate. The gun sight's cover was slightly modified. 110 were produced.

PzKpfw 38(t) Ausf C, series comprised 110 vehicles manufactured from May to August 1940. Changes included protector for the turret ring, German aerial, and moving the silencer (muffler) to the top of the rear plate.

PzKpfw 38(t) Ausf D: 105 tanks were produced between September and November 1940. No definite features are known for this model. Some reports indicate that it had a straight 30 mm driver's front plate.

PzKpfw 38(t) Ausf E was made from November 1940 to May 1941, 275 tanks were delivered. The driver's front plate and turret front were uparmoured to 50 mm. This series is easily recognized by the straight driver's plate, bolted armour on turret front, splash ring over turret machine-gun eliminated and, usually, a large stowage box on the left mud guard. Aside from 25 + 25 mm frontal armour, the side armour was increased to 15 + 15 mm, and the driver and the hull gunner were provided with new visors.

PzKpfw 38(t) Ausf F was manufactured concurrently with the Ausf S between May and October 1941, the 250 Ausf F were similar to the Ausf E with the 25 + 25 mm frontal and 15 + 15 mm side armour.

PzKpfw 38(t) Ausf S: In 1939 Sweden had ordered 90 tanks from BMM, but in 1940 work on their manufacture was suspended to allow completion of orders for the German Army. Later that year the Germans decided to confiscate the tanks for their own use, but at the same time they opened negotiations to allow Sweden licence to build the PzKpfw 38(t). The 90 vehicles, designated Ausf S were to be assembled in February 1941 but due to difficulties in converting them for German use the work did not take place until May to September. Despite being built in 1941 alongside the Ausf F these vehicles were basically similar to the old Ausf A, B or C.

PzKpfw 38(t) Ausf G was the last version of the original tank. 500 chassis were built, but only 321 were completed as PzKpfw 38(t) between October 1941 and July 1942.

The total of PzKpfw 38(t) produced was 1414 (1411 plus three prototypes). Aside from these, BMM manufactured in 1940 21 vehicles of the LT vz 40 type for the Slovak Army, and 15 TNHnA tanks in 1942. These were BMM's entry for the OKW trials for a reconnaissance tank. With the 3.7 cm gun, 35 mm armour and a new V8 engine of 250 HP, they attained speeds over 60 km/hour.

Panzerjäger 38(t) Series: The changing situation on the battle fronts in late 1941 necessitated the next conversion and gave a new lease on life to the outdated PzKpfw 38(t) tanks. The 3.7 cm guns were proven to be totally inadequate against the Russian T-34 and KV-1 tanks, but Germany at this

Table 5: Production of PzKpfw 38(t) and its Modifications

Series	Ausführung (Type)	Fahrgestell Nr. (Chassis No.)	No. of Vehicles Produced	Production Dates	Modifi- cation
I	A	0001-0150	150	First 9 – May 39, last 11 – Nov 39	
II	B	0151-0260	110	First 10 – Jan 40, last 15 – May 40	
III	C	0261-0370	110	First 15 – May 40 last 35 – Aug 40	
IV	D	0371-0475	105	First 35 – Sep 40, last 26 Nov 40	
V	E	0476-0750	275	First 1 – Nov 40, last 33 – May 41	
VI	F	0751-1000	250	First 30 – May 41, last 25 – Oct 41	
	S	1001-1090	90	First 15 – May 41, last 30 – Sep 41	
VII	G	1101-1600	500	First 28 – Oct 41, last 33 – Jul 42	321 PzKpfw 38(t) 176 7.62 cm Sfl
VIII	H	1601-2100	500	First 17 – Jul 42, last 2 – Mar 43	168 7.62 cm Sfl 242 7.5 cm Sfl 90 15 sIG Sfl
X	M	2101-	1500	First 68 – Mar 43, last 2 – Aug 44	975 7.5 cm Sfl 283 15 cm sIG Sfl
	K				140 2 cm Flak Sfl
	L				102 Mun Fzg
	K				

Series	Fahrgestell Nr. (Chassis No.)	No. of Vehicles Produced	Production Dates	Modification
Aufklärer 38(t)		70	First 37 – Feb 44, last 33 – Mar 44	Umbau (rebuilt)
Jagdpanzer 38(t) Hetzer	321001-324000	2584	First 23 – Apr 44, last 301, Mar 45	
Bergefahrzeug 38(t)		170	First 1 – Sep 44, last 21 – Mar 45	106 new, 64 Umbau
Flammpanzer 38(t)	321001-324000	20	Dec 44	Umbau
sIG 33 Sfl. auf Jagdpanzer 38(t)	321001-324000	30	First 21 – Dec 44, last 3, Feb 45	24 new, 6 Umbau
Jagdpanzer 38(t) Starr		60	1945	
PzSpähwagen II Ausf BMM (TNHnA)		15	March-August 42	
PzSpähwagen II Ausf Škoda (T-15)		1	March 42	

time had only one tank capable of carrying the long 7.5 cm gun, the PzKpfw IV.

To provide the anti-tank formations with efficient anti-tank gun on a mobile platform, the chassis of the PzKpfw 38(t) was mated, initially, with the excellent Russian 7.62 cm guns which the Germans had captured in large numbers during the Summer 1941 offensives and later with the German 7.5 cm PaK 40.

BELOW: A BMM prototype for a Panzerjäger 38(t) armed with a German gun. This protoype carried the 7.5 cm StuK 40 (L/43), as produced for the Sturmgeschütz III, but the production models of the Panzerjäger used the 7.5 cm PaK 40(L/46) which was not in such short supply by November 1942.

ABOVE: Mock-up showing a Panzerjäger 38(t) Ausf M, which was designed to carry the proposed 7.5 cm PaK L/60. This model was never produced.

Panzerjäger 38(t) für 7.62 cm PaK 36(r) (SdKfz 139) was a simple conversion. The turret and the superstructure top plate were removed and the gun mounted on a cross, whose members were welded to the hull sides and to the front and rear plates. A crudely constructed gun shield from 10 mm plate provided only a rudimentary protection for the crew. The gun had a straight sight and 30 rounds were carried in bins within the old fighting compartment. The gun was rechambered for German ammunition which gave it a muzzle velocity of 960 m/sec. It fired a 4.15 kg shell which could penetrate 94 mm armour at 1,000 m.

From April to October 1942, 344 SdKfz 139 were built, 176 on the Ausf G chassis, the rest on Ausf H with a more powerful engine, developing 140 HP at 2,500 rpm. 19 further units were converted from PzKpfw 38(t) returned to the factory in 1943.

7.5 cm PaK 40/3 auf PzKpfw 38(t) Ausf H (SdKfz 138) was a similar adaptation for the PaK 40, which had become available in May 1942. First 42 vehicles were manufactured on Ausf H chassis in November 1942. The conversion was very similar to SdKfz 139, though the gun shield was of a better design and provided more protection for the crew. The gun had a muzzle velocity of 930 m/sec and with an AP shell weighing 4.1 kg could penetrate 90 mm of armour at 1,000 m. The usual crew of four was carried. 242 vehicles of this type were manufactured between November 1942 and April 1943 and a further 175 were converted from PzKpfw 38(t) during 1943.

Panzerjäger 38(t) mit 7.5 cm PaK 40/3 Ausf M (SdKfz 138) was the final version of this series. The Ausf M chassis was originally developed as a special self-propelled carriage for the infantry howitzer by mounting the engine in the centre. The front part of the chassis was redesigned and lengthened with one straight glacis plate sloped at 67°. The driver sat on the right front side under a cast armoured hood with a hinged visor. The gun was mounted in the rear at pannier height and was protected by a four-sided superstructure. Armour on the gun shield was 10 mm, on the hull only 15 mm. Crew was again four, but three of them rode in the fighting compartment, the hull machine-gun was deleted. 27 rounds for the gun were carried. Between April 1943 and May 1944, BMM manufactured 975 vehicles of this type.

Other Modifications

15 cm sIG 33(Sfl) auf Panzerkampfwagen 38(t) Ausf H 'Grille' (SdKfz 138/1) To provide fully tracked supporting artillery for infantry formations, Alkett designed a conversion based on the PzKpfw 38(t) Ausf H chassis, using a Rheinmetall-Borsig howitzer. The gun was again located on a cross-member, bolted to the sides and front and rear plates. 25 front and 15 mm side armour protection was fashioned around the gun, running from the driver's plate nearly the whole length of the vehicle. The prototype was manufactured by BMM in October 1942 and production started in February 1943. 90 vehicles were built on the Ausf H chassis before the Ausf M chassis, developed specifically for this use, was available.

15 cm sIG 33/2 auf Selbstfahrlafette 38(t) (Sfl) Ausf K (Sd Kfz 138/1) The original order for 200 Grille was completed with 90 based on the old Ausf H chassis and 110 as originally planned on the special new Ausf K chassis. From April 1943 until September 1944 a total of 282 of these 'Grille' self-propelled guns were built.

Aufklärer auf PzKpfw 38(t) mit 2 cm KwK 38 oder 7.5 cm KwK 38 L/24 (SdKfz 140/1) After the PzKpfw II 'Luchs' was abandoned as too complicated and costly, the pressing need for a fully tracked reconnaissance vehicle was filled by adapting PzKpfw 38(t) chassis returned for rebuilding for this purpose. In February and March 1944 70 vehicles had their original turrets removed and their chassis prepared. 50 were fitted with the 2 cm Hängelafette open topped turret. 18 without turret were delivered. Only two Aufklärungspanzer armed with the 7.5 cm KwK 38 L/24 were built.

Flakpanzer 38(t) auf Selbstfahrlafette 38(t) Ausf L (Sd Kfz 140) Between November 1943 and February 1944 BMM manufactured 140 anti-aircraft tanks on the Ausf L chassis. 2 cm Flak 38(L/55) was mounted in the rear of the vehicle and was enclosed in an armoured superstructure, whose upper half could have been opened to facilitate the work of the crew and to allow greater depression for the gun.

In this configuration, the vehicle was capable of speeds up to 50 km/hour on roads and weighed 9.8 tons. Crew was 4-5 men.

Inadequate firepower was the weakness of these vehicles and in fact the last ten chassis built for this order were converted to 'Grille'.

Munitionspanzer 38(t) (Sf) Ausf K (Sd Kfz 138) Parallel with the production of the 'Grille', from January to May 1944, a total of 102 Munitions-

ABOVE: *Mörserträger 38(t) Ausf M was a new design from 1944 for supplying self propelled artillery formations, it was not adopted.*

BELOW: *This improvisation was used during the uprising in Prague, on 9 May 1945. The partisans mounted a 3 cm MK 108/38 aircraft cannon in the superstructure of a 'Grille'. Two of these guns were to be the main armament of the so called Kleiner Kugelblitz 38(t) which was under development at BMM. (S. Zaloga).*

panzer were built on the Ausf M chassis. The limited ammunition storage capacity of the 'Grille' was to be supplemented by having two unarmed Munitionspanzer to every six with sIG.

Munitionsschlepper auf Fahrgestell PzKpfw 38(t) From 1942 many obsolete tank chassis were converted in the field to auxiliary vehicles to support self-propelled gun and tank formations. With the turret removed, they weighed only 8 tons, crew was two men. Between January and May 1944

Table 6: German Production Modifications on the TNH P-S Chassis

German Type Designation	Year	No. Built (converted)	Description
PzKpfw 38(t) Ausf A-G	1939-42	1411	Basic gun tank
PzBefWg 38(t)	1939-42	c. 5 per cent	Command tank, frame aerial
SdKfz 138 PzJäg 38 Ausf H	1942-43 (43)	242 (175)	7.5 cm PaK 40/3 in open superstructure, engine in the rear, gun in front
SdKfz 138 PzJäg 38 Ausf M	1943-44	975	final version, gun in the rear, engine front
SdKfz 138/1 Geschützwagen 38 (t) Ausf H	1942-43	90	15 cm sIG 33 howitzer in open superstructure
SdKfz 138/1 Geschützwagen 38(t) Ausf K	1943-44	282	Howitzer in the rear
SdKfz 138/1 Munitionspanzer 38(t) Ausf K	1943-44	102	ammunition carrier for the Geschützwagen 38(t)
SdKfz 139 PzJäg 38(t) für 7.62 PaK 36(r)	1941-42 (43)	344 (19)	original version of open superstructure tank destroyer, using captured Russian guns
SdKfz 140 Flakpanzer 38(t)	1943-44	140	2 cm Flak 38 in the rear
SdKfz 140·1 Aufklärungspanzer 38(t)	1943-44	(70)	recce tank, 50 with 2 cm gun in a turret from SdKfz 234
PzKpfw 38(t) Schulfahrwanne	1942-43		turret removed, driver training vehicle. Late in war fitted with wood burning generators

Jagdpanzer 38(t) Hetzer	1944-45	2584	PaK 39 L/48 gun in a new superstructure, bigger engine, wider track
Bergefahrzeug 38(t)	1944-45	(64)	recovery vehicle, no gun, fitted with winch
Flammpanzer 38(t)	1944-45	(20)	modified to carry flame thrower in place of gun
sIG 33 Sfl auf Fgst Jagdpanzer 38(t)	1944-45	24 (6)	Hetzer with a 15 cm howitzer as main armament
Total		3517 (264) 2804	on PzKpfw 38(t) chassis on Hetzer chassis
Grand Total		6321 (264)	

102 new vehicles, based on the Ausf K chassis were built specially to supply the 'Grille'.

Schulfahrerwanne PzKpfw 38(t) Some of the PzKpfw 38(t) chassis were adapted for driver training by having the turret and armament removed. Towards the end of the war, some were equipped with wood burning gas generators to save precious gasoline. These generators were quite common on German civilian trucks.

A total of 3,590 PzKpfw 38(t) and modifications was manufactured by BMM before production was terminated in September 1944.

Jagdpanzer 38(t) Hetzer (Panzerjäger 38(t) für PaK 39 L/48) Originally called 'Leichtes Sturmgeschütz 38(t)', the Hetzer was based on an enlarged version of the well proven 38(t) chassis design. The suspension and running gear was enlarged by about 10 per cent to carry the increased size, but the gearbox, steering and the final drive units were unchanged. The driver's poisition was switched to the left and the armour completely redesigned. The Hetzer had a balistically very clean shape with no vertical plates. Even the lower hull plates were sloped at a reverse angle of 15^0. The front consisted of two straight plates, the lower nose plate at a reverse angle of 40^0 and the glacis plate at 70^0. The superstructure sides were angled at 40^0. All construction was welded. The gun was a modified version of the PzKpfw IV gun and was mounted at the right side of the fighting compartment. Armour thickness was 60 mm in the front, but only 20 mm on sides and rear.

The commander sat behind the gun in a recess in the engine compartment

ABOVE: One of the many Hetzer of the Czechoslovak Armoured Corps during a post-war exercise. Spare parts were not a problem and the 7.5 cm PaK 39 gun was used by the Army anyway before a standardization with the Soviet Army got under way.

and had a flat two-piece hatch. A remotely controlled machine-gun, fed from a 50 round drum, was mounted in front of gunner's hatch on the left top side.

A stronger engine was installed. It was a modified version of the old Praga 6-cylinder with a displacement of 7,750 cc, developing 158 HP at 2,600 rpm. This gave the 15.8 ton Hetzer a top speed of 38 km/hour on the road and action radius of 180 km. 41 rounds for the gun and 1,200 rounds for the machine-gun were carried. Crew was again four; commander, gunner, loader and driver.

Though it had its share of shortcomings, the Hetzer was an effective, simple and rugged vehicle. The first 23 were manufactured in April 1944 and issued to newly formed Panzerjäger Abteilungen in July 1944. The monthly production of Hetzer in BMM was high and Škoda returned to armoured vehicle manufacture when it joined in production by September 1944. Up till March 1945. a total of 2,584 Hetzers were built. Out of this number, 2,496 were actually issued to troops, including 100 delivered to the Hungarian Army. The majority of them went to PzJäg Abteilungen or Kompanies which were either parts of Infantry Divisions or were operating as independent units. The Hetzer thus became in the closing months of the war the main weapon of the German Army's anti-tank formations.

After the war, many Hetzers remained on the soil of the former Protectorate or on the factory production lines and the newly formed Czechoslovak Army had them repaired or completed and used them in anti-tank units up to the late 50s. In Czech service, the remotely controlled machine-gun was eventually deleted.

Another country which acquired Hetzer after the war was Switzerland. The Swiss G-13 had a gun with a muzzle brake and a small cupola for the commander on the left top side. Later during overhaul they were fitted with Saurer V-8 water-cooled diesel engines. The Swiss originally ordered 100 in 1946 and deliveries began in 1947. A futher 58 were then purchased and all had been delivered by 1952. These vehicles saw service until 1970.

Hetzer Modifications

Bergepanzer 38(t) Hetzer Concurrently with the production of the Hetzer, the recovery vehicle Bergepanzer was built. A total of 170 vehicles, 106 from new production and 64 converted from normal Hetzer, was produced. With a weight of 14.5 tons and a crew of four, it had a lowered super-structure, no gun and was fitted with a winch. Used by the Hetzer units as a standard recovery vehicle, it was not too successful owing to the engine being too weak for recovery purposes.

Flammpanzer 38(t) Hetzer In December 1944, 20 Hetzers were converted to flame-throwing tanks by having their guns removed and replaced with a flame-thrower. A simulated barrel was fitted on the flame-thrower, so that the vehicle would not be so easily recognizable. Weight was 15.5 tons and again a crew of four was carried. Fuel for the flame-thrower was carried internally. This conversion was specially for the Ardennes Offensive.

15 cm sIG 33/2 (Sfl) auf Jagdpanzer 38(t) Hetzer The troops continually demanded more self-propelled 15 cm sIG guns but since production of the

BELOW: G-13 tank hunters of the Swiss Army were the Hetzers. Outside changes were the addition of the muzzle brake on the gun, two aerials and a small cupola for the commander who was moved to the left side, and an anti-aircraft machine-gun mount. (Swiss Army).

ABOVE: *During the Prague uprising against the Germans 5–9 May, 1945, the insurgents used Bergepanzer taken from the production line. Used against German machine-gun positions, they were fairly effective.*

SdKfz 138/1 Ausf M had terminated in 1944, it was impossible to meet these demands. However, in November 1944 it was decided to produce a new self-propelled howitzer on the Hetzer chassis. A total of 30 of these vehicles was built between December 1944 and February 1945, 24 from new production and 6 rebuilt from Hetzer. The howitzer was carried in a heightened

BELOW: *The Flammpanzer 38(t) Hetzer was made to look like the ordinary Panzerjäger. The 14 mm flame thrower was pump driven and a fake gun barrel was fitted over its tube. Twenty vehicles were modified from ordinary Hetzer in time for the Ardennes offensive in December 1944.*

ABOVE: *Rare picture of the mock up for the Vollkettanaufklärer 38(t), with a 7.5 cm K51 (L/24) gun.*

superstructure, which otherwise followed the clean Hetzer lines. Crew again was four.

Vollkettenaufklärer 38(t) With the phasing out of most German tank chassis in 1945, only the 38(d) and 38(t) were to remain in the light class. The existing Hetzer was to continue, in various forms, and was to be a basis for a new reconnaissance vehicle. One version, completed as a prototype,

BELOW: *BMM factory photo of the prototype Vollkettenaufklärer 38(t). Note the APC prototype in the background.*

carried the short 7.5 cm K51 gun in a sloped, open top superstructure. Also there was to be a version with the 2 cm Flak 38.

Jagdpanzer 38(t) Starr Originally, the Hetzer was designed to carry a rigid (Starr) mounted gun. Rheinmetall-Borsig was developing the gun and Alkett was charged with the vehicle adaptation studies. Two guns were envisaged for this project, the 7.5 cm PaK 39 (L/48) and the 10.5 cm StuH 42 (L/28). Two prototypes on the 38(t) chassis were actually built and tested at Hillersleben. Problems with the sights and unmanageable handwheels led to the postponement of production of the Starr and the Hetzer with the normal gun mount was produced instead.

Heeres Waffenamt actually, in December 1944, placed an order for 100 vehicles with BMM. While waiting for the final weapon and mount design, BMM manufactured 60 vehicles before February 1945, when the decision was made to transfer production to Škoda. The final design of the weapon mount and sights was only sent to Prague in April 1945 and so the 60 Starr vehicles were never completed.

The production Jagdpanzer 38(t) Starr was based on the normal Hetzer. The rigid mount utilized a small ball mount. This allowed the gun to be moved towards the centre of the vehicle, reduced nose heaviness and overall weight. At 14 tons, the Starr had a maximum speed of 44 km/hour. Late production vehicles were to have been equipped with elevation stabilizer and a coaxial MG 34 mount.

Jagdpanzer 38(d) Originally long-term plans for AFV production specified that the PzKpfw IV chassis was to be replaced by the Pz III/IV chassis by mid 1945. However, in the Autumn of 1944 the production of the Pz III/IV was cancelled and Hitler ordered that all new constructions henceforward will be based on two chassis only, the 38(t) and the 38(d). The 38(t) was to continue in production at BMM and Skoda as the Hetzer, Hetzer Starr, sIG (Sf) and Aufklärer.

The 38(d) was a slightly larger redesigned version of the 38(t), differing mainly in that it used the new Tatra 12 cylinder air-cooled diesel engine, developing 220 HP, new drive train and new drive and sprocket wheels.

This redesigned vehicle was large enough to accommodate the 7.5 cm PaK 42 (L/70) and thus could replace the Pz IV/70. Alternative weapons were PaK 39 (L/48) and StuH 42, so that the vehicle could replace the StuG III as well. Only prototypes had been completed, but it was planned that from mid 1945 Alkett, Vomag, Krupp-Gruson, MIAG and Ni-Werke will be producing 1,250 units per month.

In addition to the Jagdpanzer vehicles, the 38(d) was intended as a basis for a replacement Flakpanzer Kugelblitz when the Pz IV chassis was terminated. It was to use a small turret, carrying the formidable armament of two 2 cm MK 151 cannons and two 3 cm MK 103 cannons, controlled by one crew member. The hydraulic traverse and elevation permitted 45° per second movement. This vehicle existed only as a wooden mock-up.

The Jagdpanzer 38(d) was supposed to weigh 16 tons with 80 mm frontal armour. The new engine gave it a top speed of 42 km/hour and range of 220 km on roads.

In late 1944 a specification was issued for a fully tracked personnel carrier based on the lengthened 38(d) chassis. By adding a fifth wheel, the length was increased to 6.2 m. The armour was 30 mm front and 20 mm sides. The vehicle carried a hemispherical turret with a dual-purpose 2 cm gun and had a crew of four. It could carry 8 men in the rear section. Weight was to be 12 tons and speed with the Tatra engine 30 km/hour with a range of 200 km. Again, only a mock-up was built in 1945.

Leichter Einheitswaffenträger

10.5 cm le FH 18/40/5 – GW 638/26 (Gerät 587)
15 cm sIG 33/2 – GW 638/27 (Gerät 588)

The initial large and complicated designs for Waffenträger (gun carrier) based upon the Pz III/IV chassis were built during 1943. The Wa Prüf 4 decided that these were too heavy and too costly for the purposes of the artillery. In February 1944 a new specification was issued for a Waffenträger to replace the towed artillery weapons. The gun was to be dismountable, but from a low rear platform without special equipment. With a 360° traverse, the elevation was specified at −8° +45°. Krupp was given overall responsibility for the project, including the light Waffenträger which was to be built with Pz 38(t) components with Rheinmetall co-operating on the gun and Ardelt and Steyr developing the chassis. The front drive was adopted, as it allowed a lower gun platform. Steyr proposed a vehicle with the running gear based on the RSO, but the Ardelt design based on the regular 38(t) was accepted for production. The engine and drive-train were placed to the right of the driver, whose compartment could have been folded to allow increased depression of the gun.

Prototypes were built in late 1944 based on the 38(t) chassis. In this version the vehicle with the 10.5 cm gun had a weight of 13.5 tons, length 6.35 m, width 3.16 m and armour between 10 and 20 mm. Crew was again four and the Praga engine gave the vehicle a top speed of 35 km/hour.

Production was planned for Spring 1945 with 350 units per month by September 1945. Production vehicles were planned on a chassis with the more powerful engine and new drive train of the 38 (d). A prototype of this Waffenträger based on 38(d) and mounting the 8.8 cm PaK 43 was built and successfully tested at Hillersleben as late as 27 April, 1945.

Mittlerer Einheitswaffenträger

10.5 cm le FH 18/40/5 – GW 638/21 (Gerät 578)
15 cm sIG 33/2 – GW 638/20 (Gerät 577)
12.8 cm K81/3 – GW 638/22 (Gerät 579)
15 cm sFH 18/6 – GW 638/23 (Gerät 580)

From Autumn 1944 this project was being developed simultaneously with the 'leichter Waffenträger' so as to have more possibilities for the types of guns mounted. The vehicle was larger, with 6 wheels per side, and was known as Krupp I, while the four-wheel vehicle was known as Krupp II.

Table VII: German Projects for Vehicles based on the TNHP-S Chassis

Designation	Year	Description
Morserträger 38(t)	1943	8 cm Gr W in special version of Ausf M
PzKpfw 38(t) mit turm PzKpfw IV	1944	Hetzer chassis with PzKpfw IV Ausf J turret
PzAufklwg (2 cm Flak 38)	1944	Hetzer chassis with 2 cm Flak 38
PzAufklwg (7.5 cm K 51)	1944	Hetzer chassis with 7.5 cm K 51
StuH 638	1944	Hetzer with 10.5 cm StuH 42
Jagdpanzer 38(t) Lang	1944	Hetzer with 7.5 cm PaK 42 L/70
Kleiner Kugelblitz	1944	2 x 3 cm Mk 103 and 2 x 2 cm Mk 151 guns in hemispherical rotating flakpanzer turret
PzKpfw 38(t) PaW 8 cm	1944	anti-tank rockets as main armament
PzAufklwg (2 cm 38 ZW)	1944	twin 2 cm KwK 38 turret
PzAufklwg (12 cn Gr W 42)	1944	12 cm Mortar armament
Schützenpanzer-wagen 38(t)	1945	2 cm KwK 38 armament, chassis lengthened by one bogie

BELOW: Gerät 578, or Mittlerer Einheitswaffenträger on 38(t) chassis with 10.5 cm le FH 18/40. Again, note how low the gun platform is.

ABOVE: Even the Russians used Czech tanks after capture and recovery of damaged vehicles from the battlefield. Here a couple of PzKpfw 38(t) Ausf E, formerly of the 19th Panzer Division, are being repaired, allowing an interesting view of the engine compartment.

Originally the Pz III/IV had been intended as the chassis for the Mittlerer Waffenträger.

Certain problems arose with the length to width ratio and the design had not been adopted for production before the end of the war. Prototypes were again built using the 38(t) chassis and later the 38(d), which was envisaged for production. Armour was between 10 and 20 mm and weight was dependent on the type of gun mounted. With the 10.5 cm gun it was 13 tons, with the 12.8 cm gun 15.8 tons. Mounting the 8.8 PaK was again planned.

BELOW: These two vehicles are of interest. In the foreground is an early production Hetzer which can be identified by the narrow front on the gun mantlet. In the background appears to be a Bergewagen being used as a mount for the 2 cm Flak 38. Whether this is a makeshift conversion of an example of the PzAufklwg 638/11 (2 cm Flak 38) is not known.

11. Skoda Wartime Developments

Aside from developing the S-II-c medium tank to the T-21 and eventually the T-22 for the Hungarian Turán. In 1941 Škoda submitted plans for a Selbstfahrlafette with a 10.5 cm howitzer on the chassis of the T-21 tank for the SS, who were interested in Škoda tanks. Škoda was also working on two prototypes. The T-15 was to be a fast light reconnaissance tank, very similar to the TNHnA of CKD. With a weight of 10 tons and a V8 engine it attained 56 km/hour. It was equipped with the new Škoda hydraulic steering unit, which was supposed to east the steering considerably.

The medium T-25 was a much more interesting design. It was clearly influenced by the T-34 with its sloping armour plate and turret well forward. With the 450 HP engine it had a high power/weight ratio and was supposed to attain speeds up to 60 km per hour. Škoda developed a new A-18 7.5 cm KwK gun for this tank. The gun was semi-automatic and was equipped with a drum auto-loading device and ejection of gasses by compressed air. Both these were not accepted by OKW and the T-25 did not get even past the mock-up form.

Later Škoda experimented with hydraulic gear change with pre-selector and wheel steering and was actively engaged with gasoline-electric drive units for extra-heavy tanks.

In January 1945 they had an order from OKH to develop a steam driven tracked tractor and recovery vehicle. Before the end of the war Škoda

BELOW: End of the road for the original Škoda built S-II-a/T-II PzKpfw 35(t) — a number of tanks were finally converted to ammunition carriers and artillery tractors. As a tractor, it could tow guns up to the total weight of 12 tons.

ABOVE: Škoda used the chassis of a PzKpfw 35(t) as the basis of a test vehicle which had petrol-electric drive, powered by a 220 hp air cooled radial engine. Such a configuration allowed a very clear driving compartment with steering wheel instead of levers.

finished a prototype of the Dampfschlepper, which was powered by two 112 HP steam engines, fed from a central boiler (25 atm, 320°C). The vehicle was based on the 38(d) chassis and had a weight of 20 t, speed up to 15 km/hour, radius 150 km and pulling strength of 9.2 t.

From September 1944 Škoda re-entered the AFV production tables with the Hetzer, but besides this and the few interesting prototypes described above Škoda devoted its wartime development and production to guns and artillery.

Production of guns used in the German AFVs included the 4.7 cm PaK (t), 7.5 cm PaK 39, 7.5 cm StuK 40 and 7.5 cm PaK 42. Škoda were also responsible for the development of the 15 cm StuH 43 and StuH 43/1 used on the Brummbär, the 7.5 cm KwK 42/1 for the Panther Schmal Turm, and an auto-loader for this gun. In January 1945 they commenced a design and within three months had built a prototype of a 30.5 cm Granatwerfer which was to be mounted on the Selbstfahrlafette GW 606/9 (Gerät 817) based on the Tiger B. A further design was a similar 42 cm smoothbore mortar which was to be mounted on the same chassis. They also built the multiple 10.5 cm Raketenwerfer in Kammerlafette which was to be mounted on the Panther tank chassis.

12. Bibliography

Up to the time of the publication of this work in 1979 there has been no single comprehensive history of Czechoslovak Armoured Fighting Vehicles. Most of the research material from which this book was written was collected in various archives around the World. The following list, however, indicates the various publications which carry sections dealing with or photographs of Czechoslovak vehicles.

Charles K Kliment/Hilary Louis Doyle
Armour of the Slovak State – Military Journal
Military Graphics Corp, Vermont 1978
PzKpfw 38(t) in Action
Armor Series
Squadron Signal Publications, Michigan 1979
Peter Chamberlain/Hilary Louis Doyle
Bellona Handbook No 1 Part 2 – Selfpropelled Weapons of the German Army
Weapons on Foreign Built Fully Tracked Chassis
Bellona Publications, Watford 1968
German Selfpropelled Weapons
Profile No 55
Profile Publications, Windsor 1973
Peter Chamberlain/Hilary Louis Doyle/Tom Jentz
Encyclopedia of German Tanks of World War II
Arms and Armour Press, London 1978
Chris Ellis/Hilary Louis Doyle
Panzerkampfwagen – German Combat Tanks 1933–1945
Bellona Publications, Watford 1976
Hilary Louis Doyle
Bellona Military Vehicle Prints – Series 4 Jagdpanzer Hetzer
Bellona Publications, Watford 1965
Bellona Military Vehicle Prints – Series 10 7.62cm PaK 36(r) auf PzKpfw 38(t)
Walter J Spielberger
with drawings by Hilary Louis Doyle

BELOW: An excellent 'battlefield' view of the 38 M(t) Pancelos Harckocsi (PzKpfw 38(t) Ausf G) of the Hungarian 1st Pancelos Hadosztaly during training in mid 1942. Many of these were outgunned and destroyed by heavier T-34 and KV-1s on the Don Front in 1943. (Magnuski).

Reihe Militärfahrzeuge – Band 4 Gepanzerte Radfahrzeuge
Motorbuch Verlag, Stuttgart 1974
Reihe Militärfahrzeuge – Band 8 Special Panzerfahrzeuge
Motorbuch Verlag, Stuttgart 1977
Reihe Militärfahrzeuge – Band 10 Rad und Volketten Zugmaschinen
Motorbuch Verlag, Stuttgart 1978
Reihe Militärfahrzeuge – Band 11 PzKpfw 35(t) und PzKpfw 38(t) und ihre Abarten
Motorbuch Verlag, Stuttgart 1980
Kraftfahrzeuge und Panzer des Österreichischen Heeres 1986 bis Heute
Motorbuch Verlag, Stuttgart 1976
Walter J Spielberger/Uwe Feist
Armor Series 3 – Sturmartillerie from Assault Guns to Hunting Panther
Aero Publishers, California 1967
Armor Series 4 – Sturmartillerie Selfpropelled Guns and Flak Tanks
Aero Publishers, California 1967
Peter Chamberlan/Chris Ellis
Tanks of the World 1915–1945
Arms and Armour Press, London 1972
World War II Fact Files – Axis Combat Tanks
Macdonald and Jane's London 1977
Bart H Vanderveen
The Observer's Army Vehicles Directory to 1940
Frederick Warne, London 1974
The Observer's Army Vehicles Directory of World War II
Frederick Warne, London 1972
Robert J Icks
Tanks and Armoured Vehicles 1900–1945
Philip Andrews Publishing
Vladimír Karlický
Umlcené Zbrane 1918–1939
Nase Vojsko, Praha 1966
Ceskoslovenské Delostre Lecke Zbrane
Nase Vojsko, Praha 1975
Wolfgang Venohr
Aufstand für die Tscheschoslowakei
Chriastian Wegner Verlag, Hamburg 1969
Fritz Heigl
Taschenbuch der Tanks
Lehmanns Verlag, München 1935
Horst Scheibert
Panzer 38(t) – Waffen Arsenal Band 23
Podzun Verlag, Freidburg 1976
Panzerkampfwagen Skoda 35(t) – Waffen Arsenal Band 21
Podzun Verlag, Freidburg 1976
Franz Kosar
Taschenbuch der Artillerie
Lehmanns Verlag 1971–1973
Terry J Gander
German Anti-tank Guns 1939–1945
Almark Publications, London 1973
Karl R Pawlas
Waffen Revue Nr 23
Karl R Pawlas Verlag, Nürnberg 1977
Various Authors
Articles on Czechoslovak Armoured Vehicles
AFV News
George Bradford, Ontario.

13. Specifications

Vehicle Type: Armoured Car
Manufacturer: Škoda
Manufacturer's Designation: PA-I
Year of Introduction: 1923
Czechoslovak Army Designation: NA
Number of Vehicles Produced:
   For the Czech Army; 2 prototypes
   For Export: −
Weight: 6.5 t
Length: 6.0 m
Width: 2.1 m
Height: 2.9 m
Armour: 3-6 mm
Armament:
   Main: 2 x Schwarzlose 7.92 mm vz 24
   Secondary: −
Ammunition Carried: NK
Crew: 5

Engine Type: Škoda, 4 cylinder, water cooled
Displacement: NK
Horse Power: 70
Maximum Speed: 52 km/hr in both directions
Radius of Action: 200 km
Special Features: Symmetrical construction, both axles driven and steerable. Two drivers, could be driven in both directions

BELOW: Škoda PA-I.

ABOVE: The OA vz 25 Želva.

Vehicle Type: Armoured Car
Manufacturer: Škoda
Manufacturer's Designation: PA II Želva (Turtle)
Year of Introduction: 1925
Number of Vehicles Produced:
  For Czech Army: 12
  For Export: In 1934 3 sold to Austrian Police
Weight: 7.4 t
Length: 6.2 m
Width: 2.2 m
Height: 2.6 m
Armour: 3-6 mm
Armament:
  Main: 4 x Schwarzlose 7.92 mm vz 24
  Secondary: –
Ammunition Carried: NK
Crew: 5
Engine Type: 4 cylinder, water cooled
Displacement: NK
Horse Power; 70
Maximum Speed: 70 km/hr in both directions
Radius of Action: 300 km

Special Features: No turret, rounded body with four diagonally placed heavy machine-guns in special mountings, allowing fire in all directions. Symmetrical construction, both axles driven and steerable, two drivers, could be driven in both directions

Vehicle Type: Armoured Car
Manufacturer: Škoda
Manufacturer's Designation: NK
Year of Introduction: 1929
Czechoslovak Army Designation: OA vz 29
Number of Vehicles Produced:
  For Czech Army: 1 prototype
  For Export: –
Weight: 11.0 t
Length: 6.2 m
Width: 2.2 m
Height: 2.9 m
Armour: 8-11 mm
Armament:
  Main: 75 mm Škoda field gun

BELOW: Škoda OA vz 29.

ABOVE: A combined recce group, with an OA vz 27 armoured car, a troop of motorcyclists and a utility car, in this case a Praga passenger car with a military body fitted.

Secondary: 1 x Schwarzlose 7.92 mm vz 24

Ammunition Carried: NK

Crew: 4

Engine Type: Škoda, 4 cylinder, water cooled

Displacement: NK

Horse Power: 70

Maximum Speed: 70 km/hour forward only

Radius of Action: 300 km

Special Features: Called 'gun armoured car', this was a sole prototype built by Škoda on the chassis of PA II. In a specially designed superstructure it carried a 75 mm Škoda field gun in front and a heavy machine-gun at the rear. No turret was provided. Both axles were driven and steerable as for the PA II.

Vehicle Type: Armoured Car

Manufacturer: Škoda

Manufacturer's Designation: PA III

Year of Introduction: 1927

Czechoslovak Army Designation: OA vz 27

Number of Vehicles Produced:
For Czech Army: 24
For Export: –

Weight: 6.5 t

Length: 6.2 m

Width: 2.2 m

Height; 2.83 m

Armour: 5-8 mm

Armament:
Main: 2 x Schwarzlose 7.92 mm vz 24
Secondary: –

Ammunition Carried: NK

Crew: 5

Engine Type: Škoda 4 cylinder, water cooled

Displacement: NK

Horse Power: 60

Maximum Speed: 35 km/hr in both directions

Radius of Action: 200 km

Special Features: Envisaged as a supporting armoured car, developments were planned for its up-gunning with a 14.5 mm heavy machine gun or a 37 mm anti-tank gun. As the main effort was shifted to tanks, this was never realized. Both axles driven and steerable, two drivers. In the back of the turret a searchlight was mounted. Used up to 1939.

Vehicle Type: Armoured Personnel Carrier

Manufacturer: Tatra

Manufacturer's Designation: Type 26·30

Year of Introduction: 1929

Czechoslovak Army Designation: NK

Number of Vehicles Produced:
For Czech Army: NK
For Export: –

Weight: 3.1 t

Length: 4.1 m

ABOVE: Tatra Type 34.

Width: 1.7 m
Height: 2.0 m
Armour: 8 mm
Armament:
   Main: 2 x light 7.92 mm ZB vz 26
   Secondary: –
Ammunition Carried: NK
Crew: Driver, commander plus 6 men
Engine Type: Tatra, 4 cylinder, air cooled
Displacement: 1680 cc
Horse Power: 24
Maximum Speed: 60km/hr
Radius of Action: 250 km
Special Features: Armoured personnel
   carrier, designed to carry an infantry
   half-squad and two light machine-guns.
   Open top, three axles, two of them
   driven. Utilizing standard Tatra chassis
   with a central tube and swing-out half
   axles. Acceptable cross-country
   capability.

Vehicle Type: Armoured Car
Manufacturer: Tatra
Manufacturer's Designation: Type 34
Year of Introduction; 1929
Czechoslovak Army Designation: NA
Number of Vehicles Produced:
   For Czech Army: 1 prototype
   For Export: –
Weight: NK
Length: NK
Wdith: NK
Height: NK

Armour: 6 mm
Armament:
   Main: 1 x heavy 7.92 mm machine-gun
   Secondary: –
Ammunition Carried: NK
Crew: 4
Engine Type: Tatra, 6 cylinder, water
   cooled
Displacement: 2300 cc
Horse Power: 40
Maximum Speed: 60km/hr
Radius of Action: 450 km

Vehicle Type: Armoured Car
Manufacturer: Tatra
Manufacturer's Designation: Type 72
Year of Introduction: 1930
Czechoslovak Army Designation: OA vz
   30
Number of Vehicles Produced:
   For Czech Army: 51
   For Export: From 1939 13 served with
   Slovaks
Weight: 3.6 t
Length: 4.02 m
Width: 1.52 m
Height; 2.00 m
Armour: 3-6 mm
Armament:
   Main: 2 x light 7.92 mm ZB vz 26
   Secondary: –
Ammunition Carried: NK
Crew: 3
Engine Type: Tatra, 4 cylinder, air cooled

ABOVE: OA vz 30.

Displacement: 1910 cc
Horse Power: 30
Maximum Speed: 60 km/hr
Radius of Action: 250 km
Special Features: Conventional construction with a turret, three axles, two of them driven, driveable in one direction only. Used the Tatra central tube chassis and swing-out axles, which gave it decent cross-country performance.

BELOW: KH 70.

Vehicle Type: Light Tank/Tractor
Manufacturer: Škoda & Tatra
Manufacturer's Designation: KH50, KH60, KH70
Year of Introduction: 1925
Czechoslovak Army Designation: KH50
Number of Vehicles Produced:
For Czech Army: 17 prototypes only

ABOVE: Tarčik vz 33.

For Export: Turkey – KH70
Weight: 7.5 t
Length: 4.50 m
Width: 2.30 m
Height: 2.53 m on wheels, 2.38 m on tracks
Armour: 6-13 mm
Armament:
  Main: 3.7 cm Škoda Infantry Gun
  Secondary: –
Ammunition Carried: NK
Crew: 2
Engine Type: Škoda, 4 cylinder, water
  cooled
Displacement: NK
Horse Power: 50
Maximum Speed; 35 km/hr on wheels
Radius of Action: 300 km on wheels on
  road
Special Features: The wheel-cum-track
  vehicle, prototypes only. For changing
  from wheels to track, the crew had to
  leave the vehicle and use special ramps
  the vehicle carried. This change took
  about 10 minutes. The KH 60 and KH 70
  were each powered by bigger engines.
  The artillery tractor versions had an open
  driver's cab at the front and crew
  compartment over the engine at the rear.

Vehicle Type: Tankette
Manufacturer: ČKD
Manufacturer's Designation: P-I
Year of Introduction: 1933
Czechoslovak Army Designation: Tančik
  vz 33
Number of Vehicles Produced:
  For Czech Army: 70
  For Export: From 1939 30 served with
  Slovaks
Weight: 2.5 t
Length: NK
Width: NK
Height: NK
Armour: 5-12 mm
Armament:
  Main: 2 x light 7.92 mm ZB vz 26
  Secondary: –
Ammunition Carried: NK
Crew: 2
Engine Type: Praga, 4 cylinder, water
  cooled
Displacement: 1,950 cc
Horse Power: 31
Maximum Speed: 35 km/hr
Radius of Action: 100 km
Special Features: Not a very good design,
  suitable only for reconnaissence.

ABOVE: AH-IV.

Vehicle Type: Light Tank
Manufacturer: ČKD
Manufacturer's Designation: AH-IV
Year of Introduction: 1935
Czechoslovak Army Designation: NA
Number of Vehicles Produced:
   For Czech Army: NA
   For Export: 50 — Iran designated RH
Weight: 3.9 t
Length: 3.20 m
Width: 1.79 m
Height: 1.67 m
Armour: 6-15 mm
Armament:
   Main: 1 x heavy 7.92 mm ZB vz 35, 1 light
   7.92 mm ZB vz 26
   Secondary; —
Ammunition Carried: 3000 rds
Crew: 2
Engine Type; Praga 6 cylinder, water
   cooled
Displacement: NK
Horse Power: 50
Maximum Speed: 45 km/hr
Radius of Action: 250 km
Special Features: Many interchangeable
   components with the TNH series.

Vehicle Type: Light Tank
Manufacturer: ČKD
Manufacturer's Designation: AH-IV
Year of Introduction: 1936
Czechoslovak Army Designation: NK

Number of Vehicles Produced:
   For Czech Army: NA
   For Export: 35 — Romania designated R-1
Weight: 4.2 t
Length: 3.20 m
Width: 1.79 m
Height: 1.67 m
Armour: 5-12 mm
Armament:
   Main: 1 x heavy 7.92 mm ZB vz 35, 1 x
   light 7.92 mm ZB vz 26
   Secondary: —
Ammunition Carried: 3000 rds
Crew: 2
Engine Type: Praga, 6 cylinder, water
   cooled
Displacement: NK
Horse Power: 35
Maximum Speed: 45 km/hr
Radius of Action: 250 km
Special Features: The commander's model
   had an additional cupola on the turret top.

ABOVE: AH-IV Sv.

Vehicle Type: Light Tank
Manufacturer: ČKD
Manufacturer's Designation: AH-IV Sv
Year of Introduction: 1937
Czech Army Designation: NK
Number of Vehicles Produced:
   For Czech Army: NA
For Export: 48 – Sweden designated Strv
   m/37 (2 built by ČKD, 46 assembled in
   Sweden by Oskarshams)
Weight: 4.8 t
Length: 3.20 m
Width: 1.79 m
Height: 2.05 m
Armour: 6-15 mm
Armament:
   Main: 2 x Ksp 8 mm m/39
   Secondary: –

Ammunition Carried: 3000 rds
Crew: 2
Engine Type: Scania-Vabis, 6 cylinder,
   water cooled
Displacement: NK
Horse Power: 80
Maximum Speed: 45 km/hr
Radius of Action: 200 km

Vehicle Type: Light Amphibious Tank
Manufacturer: ČKD
Manufacturer's Designation: F-IV-H
Year of Introduction: 1937-1941
Czechoslovak Army Designation: NA
Number of Vehicles Produced:
   For Czech Army: 1 prototype
   For Export: --

BELOW: F-IV-H amphibious tankette.

ABOVE: Modernised version of the A-IV-H offered by BMM in 1941.

Weight: 6.2 t
Length: 5.05 m
Width: 2.45 m
Height: 2.07 m
Armour: 6-15 mm
Armament:
  Main: 1 x heavy 7.92 mm ZB vz 37
  Secondary: –
Ammunition Carried: 4000 rds
Crew: 3
Engine Type: Praga 4 cylinder, water
  cooled
Displacement: NK
Horse Power: 120
Maximum Speed: 50 km/hr, in water 9
  km/hr

Radius of Action: 250 km
Special Features: By 1941 an improved
  model with more compact hull and
  flotation gear was tested by the Germans.

Vehicle Type: Light Tank
Manufacturer; ČKD
Manufacturer's Designation: P-II
Year of Introduction: 1934
Czechoslovak Army Designation: LT vz
  34
Number of Vehicles Produced:
  For Czech Army: 50
  For Export: –
Weight: 7.5 t
Length: 4.0 m
Width: 2.0 m

BELOW: The LT vz 34.

ABOVE: Iranian TNH tanks on parade in 1950 in Teheran. They were phased out of service in 1957.

Height: 1.8 m
Armour: 8-25 mm
Armament:
Main: 3.7 cm vz 34 (Škoda A-3)
Secondary: 2 x heavy 7.92 mm ZB vz 35
Ammunition Carried: Gun 50 rds, MG 1800 rds
Crew: 3
Engine Type: Praga, 4 cylinder, water cooled
Displacement: NK
Horse Power: 62
Maximum Speed: 30 km/hr
Radius of Action: 110 km
Special Features: Rugged, dependable. Noisy ventilator and tiring steering. Were to be reconstructed in 1938, using the TNH engine and gear-box, but only one tank reconstructed before the German occupation.

Vehicle Type: Light Tank
Manufacturer: CKD
Manufacturer's Designation: TNH
Year of Introduction: 1935
Czechoslovak Army Designation: NA
Number of Vehicles Produced:
For Czech Army: –
For Export: 50 – Iran designated TNH

Weight: 8.2 t
Length: 4.51 m
Width: 2.08 m
Height: 2.30 m
Armour: 8-25 m
Armament:
Main: 37 mm vz 34 (Škoda A-3)
Secondary: 2 x heavy 7.92 mm ZB vz 35
Ammunition Carried: Gun 60 rds, MG 3000 rds
Crew: 3
Engine Type: Praga TN 100, water cooled
Displacement: 7,000 cc
Horse Power: 100
Maximum Speed: 38 km/hr
Radius of Action: 200 km

Vehicle Type: Light Tank
Manufacturer: CKD
Manufacturer's Designation: LTH
Year of Introduction: 1937
Czechoslovak Army Designation: NA
Number of Vehicles Produced:
For Czech Army: –
For Export: 24 – Switzerland designated Pz 39
Weight: 7.5 t
Length: 4.51 m
Width: 2.00 m

101

ABOVE: LTH.

Height: 2.30 m
Armour: 8-32 mm
Armament:
  Main: 24 mm Oerlikon
  Secondary: 2 x heavy 7.5 mm Maxim
  Model 1911
Ammunition Carried: NK
Crew: 3
Engine Type: Saurer Arbon, diesel
Displacement: NK
Horse Power: 125
Maximum Speed: 45 km/hr
Radius of Action: 250 km
Vehicle Type: Light Tank
Manufacturer: CKD
Manufacturer's Designation: LTP
Year of Introduction: 1938
Czechoslovak Army Designation: NA
Number of Vehicles Produced:
  For Czech Army: –
  For Export: 24 – Peru
Weight: 7.5 t
Length: 4.51 m
Width: 2.08 m
Height: 2.30 m
Armour: 8-32 mm

Armament:
  Main: 37 mm vz 34 (Škoda A-3)
  Secondary: 2 x heavy 7.92 mm ZB vz 37
Ammunition Carried: Gun 60 rds, MG
  3000 rds
Crew: 3
Engine Type: Praga, 6 cylinder, water
  cooled
Displacement: 7,150 cc
Horse Power:: 125·2,200 rpm
Maximum Speed: 45 km/hr
Radius of Action: 250 km

Vehicle Type: Light Tank
Manufacturer: CKD
Manufacturer's Designation: LTL
Year of Introduction: 1938
Czechoslovak Army Designation: NA
Number of Vehicles Produced:
  For Czech Army: –
  For Export: 21 – Latvia
Weight: 7.2 t
Length: 4.51 m
Width: 2.08 m
Height: 2.30 m
Armour: 8-25 m

BELOW: LTP.

ABOVE: LTL.

Armament:
  Main: 20 mm Oerilikon
  Secondary: 2 x heavy 7.92 mm ZB vz 37
Ammunition Carried: NK
Crew: 3
Engine Type: Praga, 6 cylinder, water cooled
Displacement: 7150 cc
Horse Power: 125·2,200 rpm
Maximum Speed: 54 km/hr
Radius of Action: 250 km
Special Features: This was the only tank of the LT series to have a rear drive.
This series was never delivered to Lativa, but later changed to 37 mm gun and sold as LT vz 40 to the Slovak Army.

Vehicle Type: Light Tank
Manufacturer: CKD
Manufacturer's Designation: TNH Sv
Year of Introduction: 1939-40
Czechoslovak Army Designation: NA
Number of Vehicles Produced:
  For Czech Army: −
  For Export: 92 − originally meant for Sweden
Weight: 8.8 t
Length: 4.51 m
Width: 2.08 m
Height: 2.30 m
Armour: 8-25 mm
Armament:
  Main: 37 mm vz 38 (Škoda A-7)
  Secondary: 2 x heavy 7.92 mm ZB vz 37
Ammunition Carried: Gun 90 rds, MG 2550 rds
Crew: 4
Engine Type: Praga, 6 cylinder, water cooled

Displacement: 7,150 cc
Horse Power: 125·2,200 rpm
Maximum Speed: 42 km/hr
Radius of Action: 200 km
Remarks: These tanks were originally manufactured for Sweden. The gun, machine-gun and the engine would have been of Swedish manufacture. After being seized by the Germans in 1940, they were brought to the standard of the regular TNH P-S under the designation PzKpfw 38(t) Ausf S.

Vehicle Type: Light Tank
Manufacturer: Scania Vabis − Sweden
Manufacturer's Designation: NA
Year of Introduction: 1941
Swedish Army Designation: Strv m/41 S-I
Number of Vehicles Produced:
  For the Swedish Army: 116 (1 prototype delivered by BMM in June 1941)
  For Export:
Weight: 10.5 t

PzKpfw 38(t) Ausf S. ➤

ABOVE: Strv m/41 S-I.

Length: 4.54 m
Width: 2.14 m
Height: 2.35 m
Armour: 10-50 mm
Armament:
   Main: 37 mm Strv-K m·38 L/45 (Bofors)
   Secondary: 2 x 8 mm KsP m/39
Ammunition Carried: Gun 100 rds, MG 4000 rds
Crew; 4
Engine Type: Scania Vabis 1664·13, 6 cylinder, water cooled

Displacement: 7,750 cc
Horse Power: 145·2,300 rpm
Maximum Speed: 48 km/hr
Radius of Action: 180 km
Special Features: Based on the PzKpfw 38(t) Ausf G. The turret had a flat roof to accommodate the Swedish radio.

Vehicle Type: Light Tank
Manufacturer: Scania Vabis – Sweden
Manufacturer's Designation: NA
Year of Introduction: 1942
Swedish Army Designation: Strv m/41 S-II

BELOW: Strv m/41 S-II (Swedish Armour Association).

ABOVE: SaV m/43 fitted with a new gun and designated SaV 101.

Number of Vehicles Produced:
For the Swedish Army: 104 plus 18
converted to Sav m/43
For Export:
Weight: 11.0 t
Length: 4.61 m
Width: 2.14 m
Height: 2.35 m
Armour: 10-50 mm
Armament:
Main: 37 mm Strv-Km/38 L/45 (Bofors)
Secondary: 2 8 mm Ksp m/39
Ammunition Carried: Gun 100 rds, MG
4000 rds
Crew: 4
Engine Type: Scania Vabis 603·2 6 cylinder,
water cooled
Displacement: 8,470 cc
Horse Power: 160·2,300 rpm
Maximum Speed: 48 km/hr
Radius of Action: 230 km
Special Features: The S-II had a bigger
engine, carried more fuel (230 l) and had a
new turret with sloped sides to the front.

Vehicle Type: Self Propelled Gun
Manufacturer: Scania Vabis – Sweden
Manufacturer's Designation: NA
Year of Introduction: 1944
Swedish Army Designation: Sav m/43
Number of Vehicles Produced:
For the Swedish Army: 36
For Export: –
Weight: 12.0 t
Length: 4.61 m (4.81 m over gun)
Width: 2.14 m
Height: 2.30 m
Armour: 10-30 mm
Armament:
Main: 105 mm SaK m/44 L/21
Secondary: –
Ammunition Carried: 43 rds
Crew: 4
Engine Type: Scania Vabis 603·2, 6
cylinder, water cooled
Displacement: 8,470 cc
Horse Power: 160·2,300 rpm
Maximum Speed: 43 km/hr
Radius of Action: 180 km
Special Features: Totally enclosed
superstructure. First used the 293 mm
wide TNH track, but later a 'Type 2' track
365 mm wide was fitted. The original gun
had the recoil gear over the barrel, but this
was replaced by the more conventional
gun configuration.

ABOVE: TNHPS Prototype.

Vehicle Type: Light Tank
Manufacturer: CKD
Manufacturer's Designation: TNHP-S
Year of Introduction: 1938
Czechoslovak Army Designation: LT vz 38
Number of Vehicles Produced:
For Czech Army: 150 ordered, subsequently delivered to the German Army
For Export: –
Weight: 8;5 t
Length: 4.60 m
Width: 2.12 m
Height: 2.21 m
Armour: 8-25 mm
Armament:
Main: 37 mm vz 38 (Škoda A-7)
Secondary: 2 x heavy 7.92 ZB vz 37
Ammunition Carried: Gun 90 rds, MG 2400 rds
Crew: 3
Engine Type: Praga, 6 cylinder, water cooled
Displacement: 7,150 cc
Horse Power: 125 ·2,200 rpm
Maximum Speed: 42 km·hr
Radius of Action: 230 km
Special Features: The final type of the TNH series, manufactured for export since 1935. Excellent, dependable and rugged tank with a good gun. Envisaged as a replacement for the LT vz 35.

Vehicle Type: Light Tank
Manufacturer: CKD (BMM)

ABOVE: LT vz 40.

Manufacturer's Designation: –
Year of Introduction: 1940
Slovak Army Designation: LT vz 40
Number of Vehicles Produced:
For Czech Army: –
For Export: 21 – Slovakia
Weight: 7.5 t
Length: 4.20 m
Width: 1.98 m
Height: 2.16 m
Armour: 8-25 mm
Armament:
Main: 37 mm vz 38 (Škoda A-7)
Secondary: 2 x 7.92 mm CZ vz 37
Ammunition Carried: Gun 66 rds, MG 3000 rds
Crew: 4
Engine Type: Praga, 6 cylinder, water cooled
Displacement: 7,150 cc
Horse Power: 125·2,200 rpm
Maximum Speed: 47 km/hr
Radius of Action: 170 km

Special Features: At least two LT vz 40 were command vehicles which had a turret similar to the LTH, but only carried a machine-gun armament.

Vehicle Type: Reconnaissance Tank
Manufacturer: BMM
Manufacturer's Designation: TNHnA
Year of Introduction: 1942
Wehrmacht Designation: Pz Spähwagen II Ausf BMM·PzKpfw 38(t) nA
Number of Vehicles Produced:
15
Weight: 14.8 t
Length: 5.0 m
Width: 2.5 m
Height: 2.4 m
Armour: 8-35 mm
Armament:
  Main: 3.7 cm KwK 38(t) (Škoda A-7)
  Secondary: 2 x 7.92 mm MG 37(t)
Ammunition Carried: NK
Crew: 4
Engine Type: Praga, NRI V 8 cylinder, water cooled
Displacement: 14,450 cc
Horse Power: 250·2,500 rpm
Maximum Speed: 62 km/hr
Radius of Action: 150-200 km
Special Features: Was to have a 5 cm KwK 39/1 fitted.

Vehicle Type: Medium Tank
Manufacturer: ČKD
Manufacturer's Designation: V-8-H
Year of Introduction: 1938
Czechoslovak Army Designation: ST vz 39

ABOVE: V-8-H.

Number of Vehicles Produced:
  For Czech Army: 2 – 300 on order
  For Export: –
Weight: 16.5 t
Length: 5.25 m
Width: 2.25 m
Height: 2.30 m
Armour: 20-32 mm
Armament:
  Main: 47 mm vz 38 (Škoda A-9)
  Secondary: 2 x heavy 7.92 ZB vz 37
Ammunition Carried: Gun 90 rds, MG 3000 rds
Crew: 4
Engine Type: Praga, 8 cylinder, water cooled
Displacement: 14,450 cc
Horse Power: 240·2,500 rpm
Maximum Speed: 48 km/hr
Radius of Action: 150 km

BELOW: TNH nA had the larger running gear later used for the Hetzer.

107

ABOVE: S-I tankette.

Vehicle Type: Tankette
Manufacturer: Škoda
Manufacturer's Designation: S-I or
MUV-4 or T-I (after 1940)
Year of Introduction: 1932
Czechoslovak Army Designation: NA
Number of Vehicles Produced:
For Czech Army: –
For Export: Prototypes
Weight: 3.0 t
Length: 2.98 m
Width: 1.85 m
Height: 1.30 m
Armour: 4-10 mm
Armament:
Main: 2 x light 7.92 mm ZB vz 26
Secondary: –
Ammunition Carried: 3600 rds
Crew: 2
Engine Type: Škoda, boxer, 4 cylinder, air
cooled

Displacement: 2,660 cc
Horse Power: 40·2,500 rpm
Maximum Speed: 42 km/hr
Radius of Action: 200 km

Vehicle Type: Tankette
Manufacturer: Škoda
Manufacturer's Designation: S-I-P or T-2
(after 1940)
Year of Introduction: 1936
Czechoslovak Army Designation: NA
Number of Vehicles Produced:
For Czech Army: –
For Export: Prototypes
Weight: 4.6 t
Length: 3.65 m
Width: 2.03 m
Height: 1.56 m
Armour: 8-15 mm
Armament:
Main: 1 x heavy 7.92 mm ZB vz 35, 1 light

BELOW: S-I-P improved tankette.

ABOVE: S-I-D.

7.92 mm ZB vz 26
Secondary: –
Ammunition Carried: NK
Crew: 2
Engine Type: Škoda, 6 cylinder, air cooled
Displacement: 3,990 cc
Horse Power: 60·2,500 rpm
Maximum Speed: 45 km/hr
Radius of Action: 200 km

Vehicle Type: Tankette
Manufacturer: Škoda
Manufacturer's Designation: S-I-D or
T-2D (after 1940)
Year of Introduction: 1936
Czechoslovak Army Designation: NA
Number of Vehicles Produced:
For Czech Army: –
For Export: prototypes
Weight: 4.8 t

Length: 3.58 m
Width: 2.00 m
Height: 1.76 m
Armour: 8-22 m
Armament:
Main: 37 mm vz 34 (Škoda A-3)
Secondary: 1 x light 7.92 mm ZB vz 26
Ammunition Carried: NK
Crew: 2
Engine Type: Škoda, 6 cylinder, air cooled
Displacement: 3,650 cc
Horse Power: 60·2,500 rpm
Maximum Speed: 40km/hr
Radius of Action: 200 km

Vehicle Type: Tankette
Manufacturer: Škoda
Manufacturer's Designation: T-3D
Year of Introduction: 1938
Czechoslovak Army Designation: NA

BELOW: The T-3 D was sold to Yugoslavia.

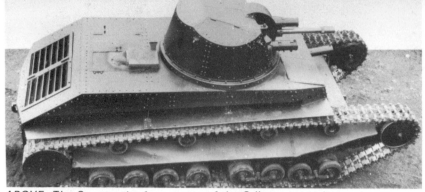

ABOVE: The Su was the forerunner of the S-II-a.

Number of Vehicles Produced:
    For Czech Army: —
    For Export: 8 (Yugoslavia – T 32)
Weight: 5.8 t
Length: 3.59 m
Width: 2.05 m
Height: 1.80 m
Armour: 5-30 m
Armament:
    Main: 37 mm vz 34 (Škoda A-3)
    Secondary: 1 x heavy 7.92 mm ZB vz 37
Ammunition Carried: Gun 25 rds, MG
    3000 rds
Crew: 2
Engine Type: Škoda diesel, 4 cylinder,
    water cooled
Displacement: 3,770 cc
Horse Power: 60·2,200 rpm
Maximum Speed: 31 km/hr
Radius of Action: 200 km

Vehicle Type: Medium Tank
Manufacturer: Škoda
Manufacturer's Designation: SU
Year of Introduction: 1934
Czechoslovak Army Designation: NA
Number of Vehicles Produced:
    For Czech Army: 1
    For Export: —
Weight: 7.5 t
Length: 4.55 m
Width: 1.90 m
Height: 1.95 m
Armour: 8-15 mm
Armament:
    Main: 37.2 mm Skoda Infantry gun
    Secondary: 2 x heavy 7.92 vz 24
Ammunition Carried: NK
Crew: 3
Engine Type: Škoda, 4 cylinder, water
    cooled
Displacement: 8,013 cc

Horse Power: 110·1,800 rpm
Maximum Speed: 30 km/hr
Radius of Action: NK

Vehicle Type: Light Tank
Manufacturer: Škoda
Manufacturer's Designation: S-II-a or T-11
    (after 1940)
Year of Introduction: 1935
Czechoslovak Army Designation: LT vz
    35
Number of Vehicles Produced:
    For Czech Army: 298 (79 used by Slovakia
    from 1939)
    For Export: 126 – Romania (R-2)
Weight: 10.5 t
Length: 4.9 m
Width: 2.1 m
Height: 2.35 m
Armour: 8-25 mm
Armament:
    Main: 3.7 mm vz 34 (Škoda A-3)
    Secondary: 2 x heavy 7.92 mm ZB vz 35
    or 37
Ammunition Carried: Gun 72 rds, MG
    1800 rds
Crew: 3
Engine Type: Škoda, 6 cylinder, water
    cooled
Displacement: 8,500 cc
Horse Power: 120·1,800 rpm
Maximum Speed: 35 km/hr
Radius of Action: 190 km

RIGHT: LT vz 35 in Czech colour scheme. ➤

ABOVE: Bulgarian PzKpfw 35(t) — Sofia 1940.

Vehicle Type: Light Tank
Manufacturer: Škoda
Manufacturer's Designation: S-II-a or T-11 (after 1940)
Year of Introduction: 1939 captured from Czech Army
German Army Designation: Panzer Kampfwagen 35(t)
Number of Vehicles Produced:
For German Army: 219
For Export: From above total – 26 – Bulgaria
Weight: 10.5 t
Length: 4.9 m
Width: 2.1 m
Height: 2.35 m
Armour: 8-25 mm
Armament:
Main: 3.7 cm KwK 34(t) (Škoda A-3)
Secondary: 2 x heavy 7.92 mm MG 35(t) or 37(t)
Ammunition Carried: Gun 72 rds, MG 1800 rds
Crew: 4
Engine Type: Škoda, 6 cylinder, water cooled
Displacement: 8,500 cc
Horse Power: 120·1,800 rpm
Maximum Speed: 35 km/hr
Radius of Action: 190 km

Vehicle Type: Medium Tank
Manufacturer: Škoda
Manufacturer's Designation: S-III
Year of Introduction: 1936
Czechoslovak Army Designation: NA
Number of Vehicles Produced:
For Czech Army: 2
For Export: –
Weight: 18.0 t
Length: 6.00 m
Width: 2.54 m

Height: 2.48 m
Armour: 16-32 mm
Armament:
Main: 47 mm (Škoda A-UV)
Secondary: 2 x heavy 7.92 ZB vz 35
Ammunition Carried: NK
Crew: 4
Engine Type: Škoda, 6 cylinder, water cooled
Displacement: 12,800 cc
Horse Power: 190·1,800 rpm
Maximum Speed: 25 km/hr
Radius of Action: NK
Special Features: Originally developed as wheel-cum-track, both prototypes were changed to fully tracked in 1936. The design was not developed further and both prototypes were scrapped in 1937.

Vehicle Type: Medium Tank
Manufacturer: Škoda
Manufacturer's Designation: S-II-c
Year of Introduction: 1938
Czechoslovak Army Designation: NA
Number of Vehicles Produced:
For Czech Army: 2
For Export: –
Weight: 16.5 t
Length: 5.56 m
Width: 2.45 m
Height: 2.37 m
Armour: 16-25 mm
Armament:
Main: 47 mm vz 38 (Škoda A-9)
Secondary: 2 x heavy 7.92 mm ZB vz 37
Ammunition Carried: Gun 80 rds, MG 1800 rds
Crew: 4
Engine Type: Škoda, V8 cylinder, water cooled
Displacement: 13,800 cc
Horse Power: 240·2,200 rpm

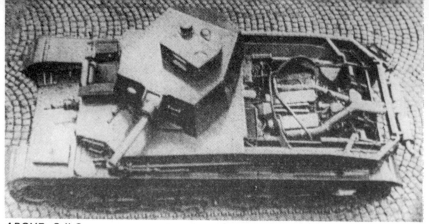

ABOVE: S-II-C.

Maximum Speed: 47 km/hr
Radius of Action: NK
Special Features: Retained the pneumatic systems of LT 35, which were perfected after several years of Army use and trials.

Vehicle Type: Medium Tank
Manufacturer: Škoda
Manufacturer's Designation: T-21
Year of Introduction: 1940
German Army Designation: NA
Number of Vehicles Produced:
 For German Army: –
 For Export: 2 prototypes
Weight: 17.0 t
Length: 5.44 m
Width: 2.45 m
Height: 2.39 m
Armour: 8-30 mm
Armament:
 Main: 4.7 cm KwK 38(t) (Škoda A-9)
 Secondary: 2 x heavy 7.92 mm MG 37(t)

Ammunition Carried: NK
Crew: 4
Engine Type: Škoda, V8 cylinder, water cooled
Displacement: 13,800 cc
Horse Power: 240·2,200 rpm
Maximum Speed: 47 km/hr
Special Features: Modified S-II-c

BELOW: Škoda used, for the first time, a V8 engine in the T-21 tanks. With a displacement of 13.8 l it developed 240 hp at 2,200 rpm.

BELOW: T-21.

ABOVE: T-22.

Vehicle Type: Medium Tank
Manufacturer: Škoda
Manufacturer's Designation: T-22
Year of Introduction: 1941
Number of Vehicles Produced:
  For Czech Army: —
  For Export: 2 (Hungary)
Weight: 18.0 t
Length: 5.44 m
Width: 2.45 m
Height: 2.39 m
Armour: 8-50 mm
Armament:
  Main: 4.7 cm KwK 38(t) (Škoda A-9)
  Secondary: 2 x heavy 7.92 mm MG 37(t)
Ammunition Carried: NK
Crew: 4
Engine Type: Škoda, V8 cylinder, water
  cooled
Displacement: 15,000 cc
Horse Power: 260·2,200 rpm
Maximum Speed: 48 km/hr
Radius of Action: —
Special Features: Uparmoured version of
  T-21. It still retained the pneumatic
  gearbox of S-II-c and T-21.

Vehicle Type: Medium Tank
Manufacturer: Škoda
Manufacturer's Designation: T-23
Year of Introduction: 1941
German Army Designation: NA
Number of Vehicles Produced: 1
Weight: 18.0 t
Length: 5.44 m
Width: 2.45 m
Height: 2.39 m
Armour: 8-50 mm
Armament:
  Main: 4.7 cm KwK 38(t) (Škoda A-9)
  Secondary: 2 x heavy 7.92 mm MG 37(t)
Ammunition Carried: NK
Crew: 4
Engine Type: Škoda, V8 cylinder, water
  cooled
Displacement: 15,000 cc
Horse Power: 260·2,200 rpm
Maximum Speed: 45 km/hr
Radius of Action: —
Special Features: Identical to T-22, but
  with a mechanical gearbox, was to have
  been fitted with the 4.7 cm KwK 41(t)
  (Škoda A-11).

ABOVE: *Turán I.*

Vehicle Type: Medium Tank
Manufacturer: M. Weiss, Magyar Waggon, GANZ, MAVAG
Manufacturer's Designation: Turan I
Year of Introduction: 1942–1944
Hungarian Army Designation: 40M Turan – Köz hk

Number of Vehicles Produced:
For Hungarian Army: 300
For Export: –
Weight: 18.2 t
Length: 5.68 m
Width: 2.54 m
Height: 2.33 m
Armour: 14-50 mm
Armament:
Main: 4 cm 41 M L/51 (Škoda A-17)
Secondary: 2 x 8 mm 34/47 M
Ammunition Carried: Gun 101 rds, MG 3000 rds
Crew: 5

Engine Type: Weiss V8 cylinder, water cooled
Displacement: 14,866 cc
Horse Power: 260·2,200 rpm
Maximum Speed: 47 km/hr
Radius of Action: 165 km

Vehicle Type: Medium Tank
Manufacturer: M. Weiss, Magyar Waggon, GANZ
Manufacturer's Designation: Turan II
Year of Introduction: 1943–44
Hungarian Army Designation: 41 M Turan Köz hk (75 Rövid)
Number of Vehicles Produced:
For Hungarian Army: 322
For Export: –
Weight: 18.5 t
Length: 5.68 m
Width: 2.54 m
Height: 2.33 m

BELOW: *Turán II which had a larger turret for its 7.5 cm gun.*

ABOVE: The prototype Turan III which had the long 7.5 cm L/43 gun and armour increased to 75 mm. Production of this tank was planned for 1944 but due to the German occupation in March 1944 only this prototype existed. The armoured apron plates were a common feature of Turan I and II which were actually used in combat.

Armour: 14-50 mm
Armament:
  Main: 7.5 cm 41 M L/25
  Secondary: 2 x 8 mm 34/37 M
Ammunition Carried: Gun 58 rds, MG 3000 rds
Crew: 5
Engine Type: Weiss V8 cylinder, water cooled
Displacement: 14,866 cc
Horse Power: 260·2,200 rpm
Maximum Speed: 47 km/hr
Radius of Action: 165 km
Special Features: Planned production of the Turan III with a 7.5 cm L·43 gun and 75 mm armour was interrupted by the German occupation in March 1944.

Vehicle Type: Assault Gun
Manufacturer: M. Weiss
Manufacturer's Designation: Zrinyi II

BELOW: Zrinyi II.

Year of Introduction: 1943
Hungarian Army Designation: 40/43 M Zrinyi Rolamlöveg
Number of Vehicles Produced:
  For Hungarian Army: 60 plus
  For Export: –
Weight: 21.5 t
Length: 5.90 m
Width: 2.90 m
Height: 2.20 m
Armour: 13-75 mm
Armament:
  Main: 10.5 cm 40/43 M L/20.5 (MAVAG)
  Secondary: –
Ammunition Carried: Gun 52 rds
Crew: 4
Engine Type: Weiss, V8 cylinder, water cooled
Displacement: 14,866 cc
Horse Power: 260·2,200 rpm
Maximum Speed: 43 km/hr
Radius of Action: 220 km

ABOVE: LKMVP.

Vehicle Type: Reconnaissence Tank
Manufacturer: Škoda
Manufacturer's Designation: T-15
Year of Introduction: 1942
German Army Designation: Pz
Spähwagen II Ausf Škoda
Number of Vehicles Produced:
1 prototype
Weight: 10.0 t
Length: 4.58 m
Width: 2.20 m
Height: 2.16 m
Armour: 8-20 mm
Armament:
Main: 3.7 cm KwK 38(t) (Škoda A-7)
Secondary: 1 x heavy 7.92 mm MG 37(t)

BELOW: Mock up of T-15.

Ammunition Carried: NK
Crew: 4
Engine Type: Škoda, V8 cylinder, water
cooled
Displacement: 10,800 cc
Horse Power: 220·2,800 rpm
Maximum Speed: 56 km/hr
Radius of Action: NK

Vehicle Type: Light Artillery Tractor,
tracked
Manufacturer: Škoda
Manufacturer's Designation: LKMVP
Year of Introduction: 1938
Czechoslovak Army Designation: NA
Number of Vehicles Produced:
For Czech Army: 1
For Export: –
Weight: 6.7 t
Length: 4.3 m
Width: 2.1 m
Height: 1.6 m
Armour: 8-15 mm
Armament:
Main: 37 mm vz 37 (Škoda A-4)
Secondary: –
Ammunition Carried: Gun 60 rds
Crew: 6
Engine Type: Škoda, 6 cylinder, air cooled
Displacement:NK
Horse Power: 105
Maximum Speed: 40 km/hr
Radius of Action: 200 km
Special Features: The vehicle carried (or
towed) the anti-tank gun and housed the
crew. The gun could be fired from the
vehicle.

ABOVE: PzKpfw 38(t) Ausf A identified by the Czech battle aerial along the hull side.

Vehicle Type: Light Tank
Manufacturer: BMM
Years of Production: 1939-1942
German Army Designation: PzKpfw 38(t)
Number of Vehicles Produced:
 For German Army: 1411 (Ausf A to Ausf G and Ausf S)
 For Export: From the above total:
 69 – Slovakia
 102 – Hungary
 50 – Romania
 10 – Bulgaria
Weight: 9.85 t
Length: 4.61 m
Width: 2.14 m
Height: 2.25 m
Armour: 10-25 mm, from Ausf E 10-50 mm

Armament:
 Main: 3.7 cm KwK 38(t)
 Secondary: 2 x 7.92 mm MG 37(t)
Ammunition Carried: Gun 90 rds, MG 2400 later 2700 rds
Crew: 4
Engine Type: Praga, EPA, 6 cylinder, water cooled
Displacement: 7.150 cc
Horse Power: 125·2,200 rpm
Maximum Speed: 42 km/hr road
Radius of Action: 250 km road, 160 km country
Special Features: Photograph shows Ausf G.

BELOW: PzKpfw 38(t) Ausf G, the last production tank.

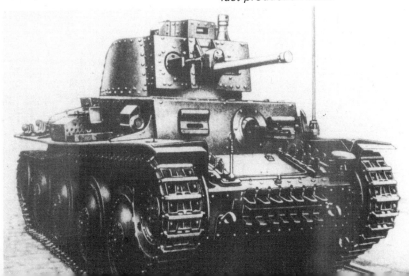

ABOVE: Panzerjäger 38(t) für 7.62 cm PaK 36(r) (Sd Kfz 139) was a simple adaptation of the 38(t) chassis to carry the Russian anti-tank gun, rechambered for German ammunition. The silhouette was quite high and crew protection minimal. This particular vehicle has the Ausf H chassis.

Vehicle Type: Tank Destroyer
Manufacturer: BMM
Manufacturer's Designation: –
Years of Production: 1941-1943
German Army Designation: Panzerjäger 38(t) für 7.62 Pa K 36(r) (SdKfz 139)
Number of Vehicles Produced:
344 (177 Ausf G plus 167 Ausf H) 19 converted from Pzkpfw 38(t) – 1943
Weight: 10.6 t
Length: 5.85 m
Width: 2.16 m
Height: 2.43 m
Armour: 15-50 mm
Armament:
Main: 7.62 cm PaK 36(r) L/51.1
Secondary: 1 x 7.92 mm MG 37(t)
Ammunition Carried: Gun 30 rds, MG 1200 rds
Crew: 4
Engine Type: Praga EPA, later EPA·2, 6 cylinder, water cooled
Displacement: 7.150 cc
Horse Power: 125·2,200 rpm, later 150·2,600 rpm
Maximum Speed: 41.6 km/hr road
Radius of Action: 284 km road, 160 km country
Special Features: Captured Russian gun, re-chambered to take German ammunition and fitted with a muzzle brake.

BELOW: Front view of the SdKfz 139. Driver's and hull gunner's compartment roof was higher and each man had his own escape hatch. The heavy imbalanced gun necessitated the massive travelling lock. This vehicle had an Ausf G chassis and it was captured in North Africa.

ABOVE: 7.5 cm PaK 40/3 auf PzKpfw 38(t) Ausf H.

Vehicle Type: Tank Destroyer
Manufacturer: BMM
Years of Production: 1942-1943
German Army Designation: 7.5 cm PaK 40/3 auf PzKpfw 38(t) Ausf H (SdKfz 138)
Number of Vehicles Produced:
 For German Army: 242
 175 converted from P2Kpfw 38t – 1943
 For Export: From the above total:
 18 – Slovakia
Weight: 10.8 t
Length: 5.77 m
Width: 2.16 m
Height: 2.50 m
Armour: 15-50 mm
Armament:
 Main: 7.5 cm PaK 40/3 L/46
 Secondary: 1 x 7.92 mm MG 37(t)
Ammunition Carried: Gun 38 rds, MG 600 rds
Crew: 4
Engine Type: Praga EPA·2, 6 cylinder, water cooled
Displacement: 7,750 cc
Horse Power: 150·2,600 rpm
Maximum Speed: 46.5 km/hr road
Radius of Action: 198 km road, 140 km country

Vehicle Type: Tank Destroyer
Manufacturer: BMM
Years of Production: 1943-1944
German Army Designation: Panzerjäger 38(t) mit 7.5 cm PaK 40/3 Ausf M (SdKfz 138)

Number of Vehicles Produced:
 For German Army: 975
Weight: 10.5 t
Length: 4.92 m
Width: 2.13 m
Height: 2.48 m
Armour: 10-15 mm
Armament:
 Main: 7.5 cm PaK 40/3 L/46
 Secondary: 1 x 7.92 mm MG 34 carried inside the vehicle
Ammunition Carried: Gun 27 rds, MG 1500 rds
Crew: 4
Engine Type: Praga, EPA·2, 6 cylinder, water cooled
Displacement: 7,750 cc
Horse Power: 150·2,600 rpm
Maximum Speed: 46.5 km/hr road
Radius of Action: 198 km road, 140 km country

BELOW: Pzjäger 38(t) mit 7.5 cm PaK 40/3 Ausf M.

ABOVE: 15 cm sIG 33(Sfl) auf PzKpfw 38(t) Ausf H.

Vehicle Type: Assault Howitzer
Manufacturer: BMM-Alkett
Years of Production: 1943
German Army Designation: 15 cm sIG 33(Sfl) auf PzKpfw 38(t) Ausf H (SdKfz 138|1)
Number of Vehicles Produced:
For German Army: 90 plus 1 prototype
Weight: 11.5 t
Length: 4.61 m
Width: 2.15 m
Height: 2.40 m
Armour: 14.5-50 mm
Armament:
Main: 15 cm sIG L/11 (Infantry howitzer)
Secondary: 1 x 7.92 mm MG 34 carried inside the vehicle
Ammunition Carried: Gun 15 rds
Crew: 5
Engine Type: Praga EPA, 6 cylinder, water cooled
Displacement: 7,150 cc

Horse Power: 125·2,200 rpm
Maximum Speed: 35 km/hr road
Radius of Action: 185 km road, 140 km country

Vehicle Type: Assault Howitzer
Manufacturer: BMM-Alkett
Years of Production: 1943-1944
German Army Designation: 15 cm sIG 33/2 auf Selbstfahrlafette 38(t) (Sf) Ausf K (SdKfz 138·1)
Number of Vehicles Produced: 282
Weight: 12.7 t
Length: 5.01 m
Width: 2.15 m
Height: 2.46 m
Armour: 10-15 mm
Armament:
Main: 15 cm sIG 33/2 L/11 (Infantry Howitzer)
Secondary: 1 x 7.92 mm MG 34 carried inside the vehicle

BELOW: 15 cm sIG 33/2 auf Sfl 38(t) Ausf K.

Ammunition Carried: Gun 18 rds
Crew: 5
Engine Type: Praga EPA·2, 6 cylinder, water cooled
Displacement: 7,750 cc
Horse Power: 150·2,600 rpm
Maximum Speed: 35 km/hr road
Radius of Action: 185 km road, 140 km country

Vehicle Type: Reconnaissence Tank
Manufacturer: BMM
Years of Production: 1944
German Army Designation: Aufklärer auf Fgst PzKpfw 38(t) mit 2 cm KwK 38 oder 7.5 cm KwK 38 L/24 (SdKfz 140·1)
Number of Vehicles Produced:
70 PzKpfw 38(t) chassis converted, 50 fitted with the 2 cm and 2 with the 7.5 cm L/24
Weight: 9.75 t
Length: 4.51 m
Width: 2.14 m
Height: 2.18 m
Armour: 10-50 mm
Armament:
Main: 2 cm KwK 38 L·55
Secondary: 7.92 MG 34
Ammunition Carried: NK
Crew: 4
Engine Type: Praga, EPA·2, 6 cylinder, water cooled
Displacement: 7,750 cc
Horse Power: 150·2,600 rpm
Maximum Speed: 52 km/hr road
Radius of Action: 240 km road, 160 km country
Special Features: PzKpfw 38(t) with the turret used for the SdKfz 234/1, and other German reconnaissance vehicles. This turret was designated 2 cm Hängelafette 38.

ABOVE AND BELOW:
Aufklärer auf Fgst PzKpfw 38(t) mit 2 cm KwK 38.

121

ABOVE: Flakpanzer 38(t).

Vehicle Type: Anti-aircraft Tank
Manufacturer: BMM
Years of Production: 1943-1944
German Army Designation: Flakpanzer 38(t) auf Selbstfahrlafette 38(t) Ausf M (SdKfz 140)
Number of Vehicles Produced: 140
Weight: 9;8 t
Length: 4.86 m
Width: 2.14 m
Height: 2.25 m
Armour: 10-15 mm
Armament:
Main: 2 cm Flak 38 L/55
Ammunition Carried: 1040 rds
Crew: 4-5
Engine Type;: Praga EPA·2, 6 cylinder, water cooled
Displacement: 7,750 cc
Horse Power: 150·2,600 rpm
Maximum Speed: 50 km·hr road
Radius of Action: 220 km road, 130 km country

Vehicle Type: Tank Destroyer
Manufacturer: BMM, Skoda
Years of Production: 1944-1945
German Army Designation: Jagdpanzer 38(t) Hetzer
Number of Vehicles Produced: 2,584
Weight: 15.8 t
Length: 4.80 m (6.38 m with gun)
Width: 2.62 m
Height: 2.17 m
Armour: 10-60 mm
Armament:
Main: 7.5 cm PaK 39 L/48
Secondary: 7.92 mm MG 34 or 42, remote controlled on roof
Ammunition Carried: Gun 41 rds, MG 1200 rds
Crew: 4
Engine Type: Praga AC·2, 6 cylinder, water cooled
Displacement: 7,750 cc
Horse Power: 158·2,600 rpm
Maximum Speed: 38.5 km·hr road
Radius of Action: 177 km road, 100 km country
Special Features: The running gear of the Hetzer, including wheels, was about 10 per cent larger with a track width of 350 mm to carry the bigger hull than had existed with the TNHP-S vehicles.

BELOW: Jagdpanzer 38(t) Hetzer.

ABOVE: Bergepanzer 38(t) Hetzer.

Vehicle Type: Recovery Vehicle
Manufacturer: BMM
Years of Production: 1944-1945
German Army Designation: Bergepanzer
38(t) Hetzer
Number of Vehicles Produced: 106 ₃ 64
modified from production Hetzer
Weight: 14.5 t
Length: 4.87 m
Width: 2.62 m
Height: 1.10 m
Armour: 20-60 mm
Armament:
Main: 7.92 mm MG 34 or 42
Ammunition Carried: NK
Crew: 4
Engine Type: Praga AC·2, 6 cylinder, water
cooled
Displacement: 7,750 cc
Horse Power: 158·2,600 rpm
Maximum Speed: 42 km/hr road
Radius of Action: 190 km rd, 120 km
country
Special Features: Fitted with electrical
winch.

*BELOW: Flammpanzer 38(t)
Hetzer.*

Vehicle Type: Flame-throwing Tank
Msnufacturer: BMM
Years of Production: 1944
German Army Designation: Flammpanzer
38(t) Hetzer
Number of Vehicles Produced: 20
(modified from production Hetzer)
Weight: 15.5 t
Length: 4.87 m
Width: 2.62 m
Height: 2.17 m
Armour: 10-60 mm
Armament:
Main: Flame-thrower, 14 mm ID, pump
driven
Secondary: 7.92 mm MG 34 or 42,
remote controlled on roof
Ammunition Carried: Fuel capacity 700 l,
mg 1200 rds
Crew: 4
Engine Type: Praga AC·2, 6 cylinder, water
cooled
Displacement: 7,750 cc
Horse Power: 158·2,600 rpm
Maximum Speed: 42 km/hr road
Radius of Action: 180 km road, 110 km
country

ABOVE: 15 cm sIG 33/2 (Sf) auf Jagdpanzer 38(t) Hetzer.

Vehicle Type: Assault Howitzer
Manufacturer: BMM
Years of Production: 1944-1945
German Army Designation: 15 cm sIG 33/2 (Sf) auf Jagdpanzer 38(t) Hetzer
Number of Vehicles Produced: 24 new, 6 rebuilt from Hetzer
Weight: 16.5 t
Length: 4.87 m
Width: 2.62 m
Height: 2.40 m
Armour: 10-60 mm
Armament:
Main: 15 cm sIG 33/2 L/11 Infantry Howitzer
Secondary: 7.92 MG 42 carried inside the vehicle
Ammunition Carried: Gun 15 rds
Crew: 5
Engine Type: Praga AC·2, 6 cylinder, water cooled
Displacement: 7,750 cc
Horse Power: 158·2,600 rpm
Maximum Speed: 42 km·hr road
Radius of Action: 130 km road, 110 km country

Vehicle Type: Tank Hunter
Manufacturer: BMM and Škoda
Years of Production: 1945
German Army Designation: Jagdpanzer 38(t) Starr
Number of Vehicles Produced: 60 awaiting completion of rigid gun mount
Weight: 14.0 t
Length: 6.38 m
Width: 2.63 m
Height: 2.17 m
Armour: 10-60 mm
Armament:
Main: 7.5 cm PaK 39/1 (L/48) in rigid mount

Secondary: 7.92 mm MG 42, remote controlled on roof
Ammunition Carried: Gun 41 rds, MG 1200 rds
Crew: 4
Engine Type: Praga AC-2, 6 cylinder, water cooled
Displacement: 7,750 cc
Horse Power: 158·2,600 rpm
Maximum Speed: 44 km/hr road
Radius of Action: 177 km road
Special Features: Rigid mounted gun in the centre of the vehicle's front plate, coaxial machine-gun was planned.
Remarks: 100 vehicles ordered in December 1944, but only 60 manufactured (and not finished) in 1945, as the final design for the gun reached Prague in late April 1945.

Vehicle Type: Tank Hunter
Manufacturer: (Planned from mid 1945) Alkett, Vomag, Krupp-Gruson, MIAG, and Nibelungenwerke
Years of Production: –
German Army Designation: Jagdpanzer 38(d)
Number of Vehicles Produced: prototypes only
Weight: 16.0 t
Length: 5.27 m
Width: 2.81 m
Height: 1.75 m
Armour: 20-80 mm
Armament:
Main: 7.5 cm PaK 42 (L/70) or 10.5 cm StuH 42
Secondary: 7.92 mm MG 42, coaxial
Ammunition Carried: NK
Crew: 4

Engine Type: Tatra 103, air cooled, V12, diesel
Displacement: 14,825 cc
Horse Power: 220·2,250 rpm
Maximum Speed: 42 km·hr
Radius of Action: 220 km road
Special Features: Larger version of the Hetzer, with new engine and drive-train, capable of mounting larger or rigid guns, planned as replacement of PzKpfw IV and StuG III.

Vehicle Type: Self propelled Gun Carrier
Manufacturer: Ardelt
Years of Production: 1944-1945
German Army Designation: Leichter Einheitswaffenträger
Number of Vehicles Produced: prototypes only
Weight: 13. 5 t
Length: 6.35 m
Width: 3.16 m
Height: 2.25 m
Armour: 10-20 mm
Armament:
Main: 10.5 cm leFH 18/40/5 or 15 cm sIG 33/2 or 8.8 cm PaK 43
Ammunition Carried: 34-96 rds, depending on gun

Crew: 4
Engine Type: Praga AC·2
Displacement: 7,750 cc
Horse Power: 158·2,600 rpm
Maximum Speed: 35 km·hr
Radius of Action: 200-220 km road
Remarks: Also known as Krupp II Waffenträger.

Vehicle Type: Self-propelled Gun Carrier
Manufacturer: Krupp
Years of Production: 1944-1945
German Army Designation: Mittlerer Einheitswaffenträger
Number of Vehicles Produced: prototypes only
Weight: 13.0 t
Length: 6.75 m
Width: 3.16 m
Height: 2.25 m
Armour: 10-20 mm
Armament:
10.5 cm leFH 18/40/5, 15 cm sIG 33/2, 10.5 cm sK 18/1, 12.8 cm K 81/3, 15 cm sFH 18·6 or 8.8 cm PaK 43
Ammunition Carried: 20-40 rds, depending on gun used
Crew: 4
Engine Type: Tatra 103, air cooled, V12 diesel
Displacement: 14,825 cc
Horse Power: 220·2,250 rpm
Maximum Speed: 35 km/hr road
Radius of Action: NK
Special Features: Lengthened version of the Leichter Einheitswaffenträger, 6 wheels per side, known as Krupp I.

LEFT AND BELOW: Leichter Einheitswaffenträger.

ABOVE: Breitfeld-Daněk 25 PS.

Remarks: Problems with length to width ratio delayed testing.

Vehicle Type: Artillery Tractor
Manufacturer: Breitfeld-Daněk (later ČKD)
Manufacturer's Designation: 25PS Schlepper
Year of Introduction: 1925
Czechoslovak Army Designation: NA
Number of Vehicles Produced:
 For Czech Army: NK
 For Export: –
Weight: 3.0 t
Length: 3.30 m
Width: 1.46 m
Height: 2.20 m
Armour: Nil
Crew: 2
Engine Type: 4 cylinder, water cooled
Displacement: 3,817 cc
Horse Power: 25

Maximum Speed: 12 km/hr
Radius of Action: NK

Vehicle Type: Artillery Tractor
Manufacturer: Škoda
Manufacturer's Designation: MTH
Year of Introduction: 1935
Czechoslovak Army Designation: NA
Number of Vehicles Produced:
 For Czech Army: 54
 For Export: –
Weight: 2.5 t
Length: 3.16 m
Width: 1.67 m
Height: 1,51 m
Armour: Nil
Crew: 4
Engine Type: Škoda, 2 cylinder, water cooled
Displacement: 2,760 cc
Horse Power: 36·1,800 rpm

BELOW: MTH.

ABOVE: T III.

Maximum Speed: 12.5 km·hr
Radius of Action: 27 km

Vehicle Type: Artillery Tractor
Manufacturer: ČKD·BMM
Manufacturer's Designation: Praga T III
Years of Production: 1938-1943
German Army Designation: leichter
  Raupenschlepper T-3-III(t)
Number of Vehicles Produced: 126
Weight: 3.9 t
Length; 3.95 m
Width: 1.73 m
Height: 2.26 m
Armour: Nil
Crew: 5
Engine Type: Praga, 6 cylinder, water
  cooled

Displacement: 4,390 cc
Horse Power: 77·2,200 rpm
Maximum Speed: 51 km·hr
Radius of Action: 260 km
Special Features: Could tow guns up to 1.8
  t weight and carry up to 600 kg.

Vehicle Type: Artillery Tractor
Manufacturer: ČKD
Manufacturer's Designation: Praga T IV
Years of Production: 1938-1939
Czechoslovak Army Designation: NA
Number of Vehicles Produced:
  For Czech Army: 25
  For Export: –
Weight: 5.07 t
Length: 4.15 m
Width: 1.67 m

BELOW: T IV.

ABOVE: T V.

Height: 2.18 m
Armour: Nil
Crew; 6
Engine Type: Praga, 4 cylinder, water cooled
Displacement: 6,080 cc
Horse Power: 56·1,300 rpm
Maximum Speed: 21 km·hr
Radius of Action: 200-220 km
Special Features: Could tow guns up to 4 t weight and carry up to 1 t.

Vehicle Type: Artillery Tractor
Manufacturer: ČKD
Manufacturer's Designation: Praga T V
Year of Introduction: 1938
Czechoslovak Army Designation: –
Number of Vehicles Produced:
    For Czech Army: –
    For Export: ? Dutch East Indies Army. Some also used by the German Army
Weight: 5.0 t
Length: NK
Width: NK

Height: NK
Armour: Nil
Crew: 5
Engine Type: Praga, 6 cylinder, water cooled
Displacement: 7,750 cc
Horse Power: 90·1,800 rpm
Maximum Speed: 30 km·hr
Radius of Action: 220 km

Vehicle Type: Artillery Tractor
Manufacturer: ČKD/BMM
Manufacturer's Designation: Praga T VI
Year of Introduction: 1937-1944
Czechoslovak Army Designation: –
Number of Vehicles Produced:
    For Czech Army: –
    For Export: 221 plus T VI-B/T VI-R-P Romania
    19 plus T VI-T Turkey
    ? T VI-P Portugal
    ? T VI-Sv Sweden
    30 T VI Slovakia
Weight: 6.85 t

BELOW: T VI.

ABOVE: T 6-SS (t)

Length: 4.80 m
Width: 1.80 m
Height: 2.42 m
Armour: Nil
Crew: 5 to 8
Engine Type: Praga TN, 6 cylinder water cooled
Displacement: 7,800 cc
Horse Power: 75·1,800 rpm
Maximum Speed: 25 km·hr
Radius of Action: 200 km
Special Features: Designed as a medium artillery tractor to tow guns of up to 6 tons weight and carry 0.8 tons payload. The T VI-Sv and vehicles built after 1940 had the Praga AE OHV engine which was 7,750 cc and developed 110/1,800 rpm. So speed and fuel consumption improved to 31 km·hr and 250 km.

Vehicle Type: Artillery Tractor
Manufacturer: BMM
Manufacturer's Designation: Praga T VI-SS
Years of Production: 1944
German Army Designation: mittlerer Raupenschlepper T 6-SS (t)
Number of Vehicles Produced: 73
Weight: 7.5 t
Length: 5.1 m
Width: 2.0 m
Height: 2.5 m
Armour: Nil
Crew: 8
Engine Type: Praga AE, 6 cylinder, water cooled
Displacement: 7,750 cc
Horse Power: 110·1,800 rpm
Maximum Speed: 31 km/hr
Radius of Action: 250 km
Special Features: Could two guns up to 6 t weight and carry up to 1 t.

Vehicle Type: Artillery Tractor
Manufacturer: BMM
Manufacturer's Designation: Praga T IX
Years of Production: 1938-1943
German Army Designation: schwerer Raupenschlepper T9
Number of Vehicles Produced: 76

BELOW: T 9.

ABOVE: A Praga T IX artillery tractor in service with the Germans. Here it is being used to tow a trailer carrying the armoured observation post which will be concreted into a large fortification. (Bundesarchiv).

Weight: 10.1 t
Length: 5.60 m
Width: 2.45 m
Height: 2.54 m
Armour: Nil
Crew: 8
Engine Type: Praga V8, water cooled

Displacement: 14,230 cc
Horse Power: 140·1,500 rpm
Maximum Speed: 20 km/hr
Radius of Action: 120 km
Special Features: Could tow guns up to 15 t weight and carry up to 1 t.

BELOW: Skoda STH medium artillery tractor was not adopted.

14. Scale Drawings

1:76 scale (4 mm = 1 ft)

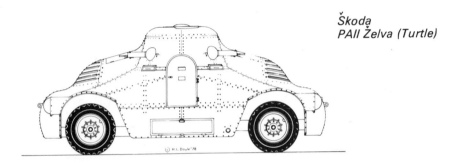

Škoda
PAII Želva (Turtle)

Tatra
Type 72 OA vz 30

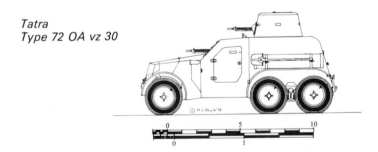

ČKD AH-IV (R-1)

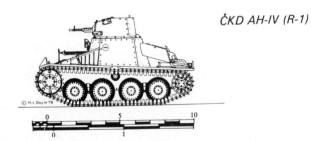

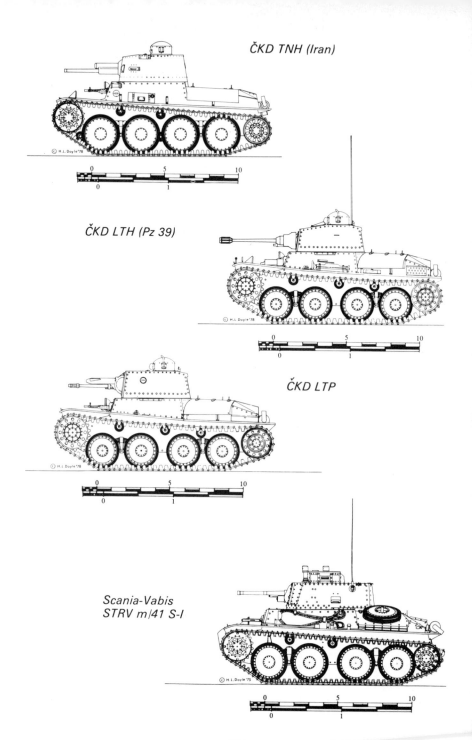

ČKD TNH (Iran)

ČKD LTH (Pz 39)

ČKD LTP

Scania-Vabis
STRV m/41 S-I

132

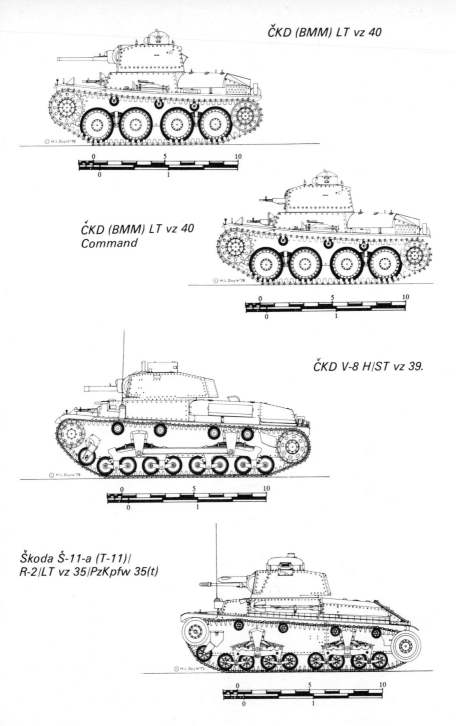

ČKD (BMM) LT vz 40

ČKD (BMM) LT vz 40
Command

ČKD V-8 H/ST vz 39.

Škoda Š-11-a (T-11)/
R-2/LT vz 35/PzKpfw 35(t)

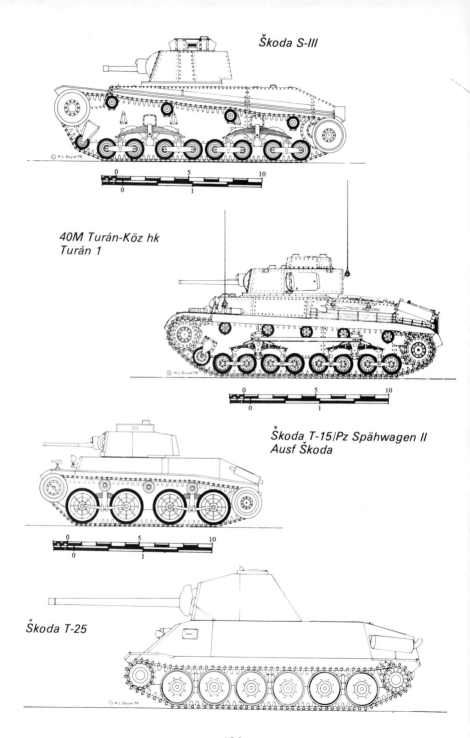

Škoda S-III

40M Turán-Köz hk
Turán 1

Škoda T-15/Pz Spähwagen II
Ausf Škoda

Škoda T-25

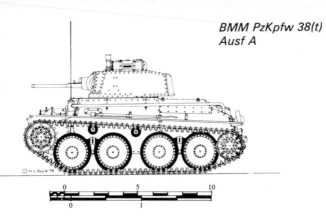

BMM PzKpfw 38(t)
Ausf A

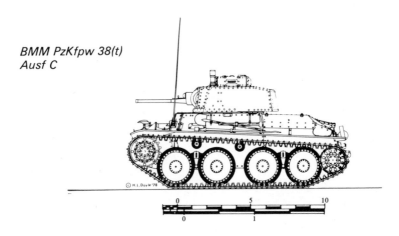

BMM PzKfpw 38(t)
Ausf C

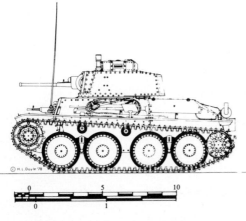

BMM PzKpfw 38(t) Ausf G

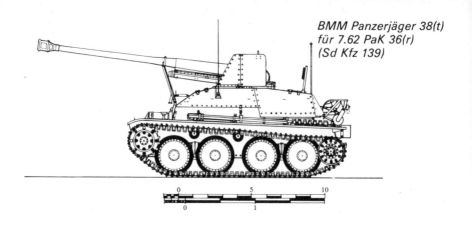

BMM Panzerjäger 38(t)
für 7.62 PaK 36(r)
(Sd Kfz 139)

0   5   10
0   1

BMM 7.5 cm PaK 40/3 auf PzKpfw 38(t)
Ausf H (Sd Kfz 138)

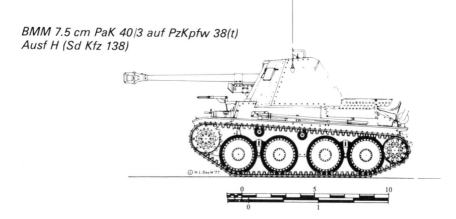

© H.L.Doyle '77

0   5   10
0   1

BMM Panzerjäger 38(t)
mit 7.5 cm PaK 40/3
Ausf M (Sd Kfz 138)

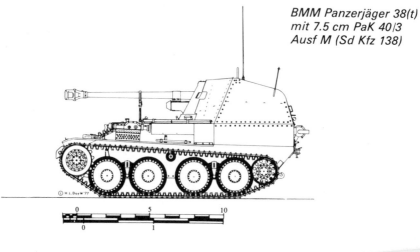

© H.L.Doyle '77

0   5   10
0   1

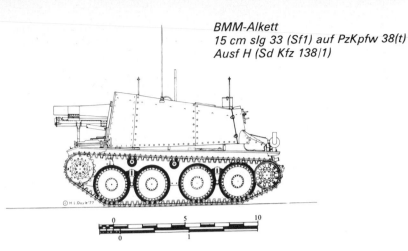

BMM-Alkett
15 cm slg 33 (Sf1) auf PzKpfw 38(t)
Ausf H (Sd Kfz 138/1)

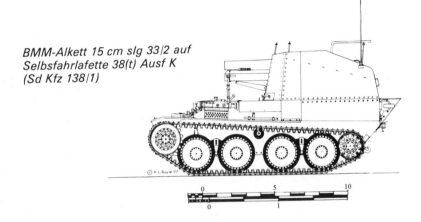

BMM-Alkett 15 cm slg 33/2 auf
Selbsfahrlafette 38(t) Ausf K
(Sd Kfz 138/1)

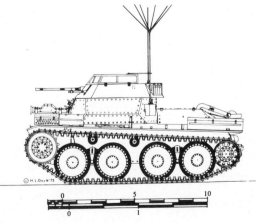

BMM Flakpanzer 38(t)
auf Selbsrfahrlafette
38(t) Ausf M
(Sd Kfz 140)

137

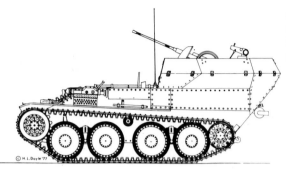

BMM Flakpanzer 38(t)
auf Selbsrfahrlafette
38(t) Ausf L
(Sd Kfz 140)

BMM, Škoda Jagdpanzer 38(t)
Hetzer

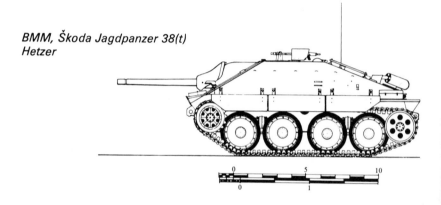

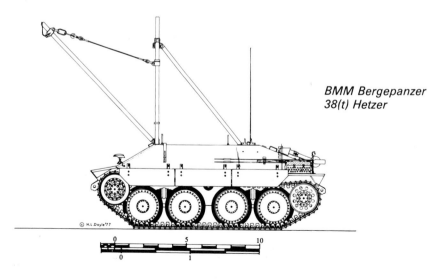

BMM Bergepanzer
38(t) Hetzer

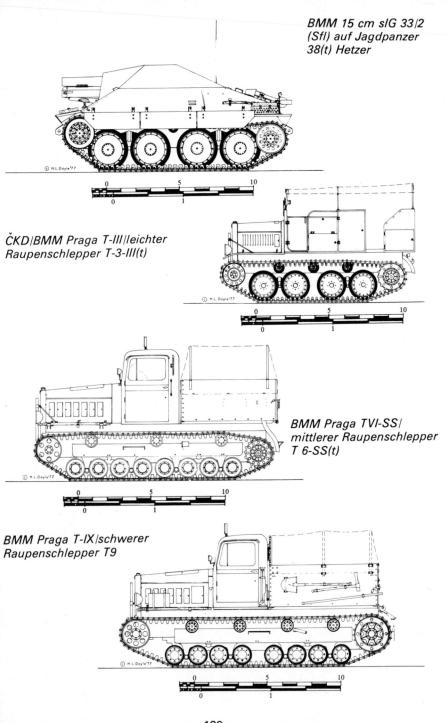

BMM 15 cm slG 33/2
(Sfl) auf Jagdpanzer
38(t) Hetzer

ČKD/BMM Praga T-III/leichter
Raupenschlepper T-3-III(t)

BMM Praga TVI-SS/
mittlerer Raupenschlepper
T 6-SS(t)

BMM Praga T-IX/schwerer
Raupenschlepper T9